THEORIES OF MASS COMMUNICATION

THEORIES OF
MASS COMMUNICATION

---

by MELVIN L. DE FLEUR

WASHINGTON STATE UNIVERSITY

SECOND EDITION

DAVID McKAY COMPANY, Inc.   NEW YORK

THEORIES OF MASS COMMUNICATION

COPYRIGHT © 1966 AND 1970
BY DAVID MCKAY COMPANY, INC.

Second Edition 1970

LIBRARY OF CONGRESS CATALOG CARD NUMBER: 74-112656

MANUFACTURED IN THE UNITED STATES OF AMERICA

TO MY STUDENTS

*from whom I received
much more than I gave*

TABLE OF CONTENTS

TABLES

TABLES

FIGURES

PREFACE

THE STUDY of mass communication seems to be emerging as a new academic discipline in its own right, although at this point it is by no means clear what its eventual organization, boundaries, and destinies will be. In the past, the content of the field and the directions of its inquiry have been defined by whatever happened to be currently capturing the attention of its more prominent students. To some extent this continues to be true at present.

But aside from contemporary fads and fancies, many rather critical issues as to the proper study of mass communication remain unresolved. For example, is it to be concerned only with the study of *mass* communication, or will it include the investigation of communication processes in general? Is it to include mainly a scientific approach, or will representatives of the humanities and arts be equal partners? These questions are more than points of abstract debate. They not only pose important issues for authors of books on mass communication, but the way in which they are eventually answered will strongly influence academic training and the professional orientations of specialists in the new field. These in turn will set the directions of research and ultimately determine the content of the accumulated knowledge about mass communication as it continues to be developed.

The characteristics which this field has had in the past are no sure guide to its future. The methodological and theoretical underpinnings of the growing discipline were forged in the behavioral sciences. Important substantive contributions have come from the communication arts and the several fields of applied communication. These various sources have yielded an amazingly diverse set of trends, specialized interests, sub-areas, and directions. In fact, the very heterogeneity of the field has sometimes proved to be an embarrassment of riches. No one has been sure at any given time, or can be sure at the present time, just what constitutes the study of mass communication.

To some this diversity may represent confusion, or the inability of students of communication to make up their minds what they should study. But lay critics often make shallow judgments. Because of their own lack of understanding of the broadly interdisciplinary nature of the field, some have concluded that mass communication is hopelessly vague and befuddled not only as to its own boundaries, but in general as an area of academic study and research.

While there can be no denying that heterogeneity exists, it is superficial thinking indeed to conclude that therefore investigators of mass communication are less capable in their research, more indecisive in choosing directions and modes of inquiry, or less worthy of support, than are individuals who study some other phenomenon. The great diversity characteristic of this area of study has come because of the utterly fundamental nature of the communication process itself, and the tremendous importance which mass communication plays in modern society. No student of human nature, whatever his disciplinary identification or theoretical orientation, can study human behavior without recognizing at the outset that Man's communication processes are as vital to him as a human being as are his biological processes. It is the latter which permit him to function as a living creature, but it is surely the former which permit him to function as a *rational* creature. It is the principles of human communication and not the principles of biological functioning that most sharply distinguish man from other living organisms.

Furthermore, it has been long recognized that interpersonal communication processes are essential to the formation and functioning of human groups both large and small. The modern urban industrial society could not exist as a social system without mass communication. It has become a deeply established part of every major social institution —political, economic, religious, educational and familial—as these sociocultural patterns have taken shape in the advanced societies of the world.

If the field of mass communication seems to be widely inclusive, then, or if there does not seem to be any sharp line of demarcation which separates it from other fields which study mankind, it is because

it occupies such a central place in the attentions of many disciplines
but is not the exclusive property of any. It is because of this that it
has developed its many trends, many interests, and many directions.
To conclude that such an important area of knowledge should make
its boundaries more rigid or should concentrate upon a narrower set of
problems is simply to ignore the importance of the communication
processes to such a wide variety of interests.

Yet, in spite of the forces for diversity and the advisability of keeping the boundaries of the field open-ended, there is a growing need to
begin some type of theoretical integration. This does not imply that the
interests of many fields should not be represented; it simply suggests
that there are certain persistent problems which seem to lie at the *center*
of almost everyone's interest. Further systematic study of these common
problems can best proceed by pulling together the ideas, concepts, and
accumulated findings that now exist into some organized framework.
Such integration would have the merit of pointing to those problems
which have been studied the most and those which have been studied
the least, and of suggesting lines of inquiry that will aid in bringing a
more balanced theoretical perspective into the field in the future.

The present small book is only a start in that direction. It is a very
modest start for several reasons. Aside from the limitations of its
author, the field of mass communication itself is barely approaching the
point where theoretical integration can begin. In fact, it is probably one
of the least theoretical areas of study that occupies the attention of
present-day writers and analysts. To be sure, it shares with its parent
disciplines an interest in behavioral theory in general, but within mass
communication as such few theoretical formulations of any sophistication have been attempted.

In spite of these inadequacies, and in the face of the old adage concerning who rushes in where angels fear to tread, the present work
has as one of its goals the focusing of attention on certain central
theoretical problems which repeatedly have served as departures for
investigation and inquiry within the field of mass communication. It
must be fully recognized that the goal of the book is more to call attention to promising directions for theoretical integration than actually to
achieve it. The latter, realistically, cannot be adequately done at the
present time.

A second and equally important goal of the present work is a purely
selfish one. It is intended to provide my own students with a guide and
overview of the field of mass communication by presenting it in a way
which has not previously been done. Thus far, most publications in

this field have been either books of readings or research monographs. With a few notable exceptions, authors have seldom attempted to provide students with broad theoretical perspectives.

To some readers this book may seem heavily concerned with some problems which are important, but concerned very little with others which may be of equal importance. This may be the case, but it was done intentionally. For example, considerable attention has been given to the historical development of the media in the American society. This has been done for two reasons. First, a theoretical problem of deep significance is concerned with the ways in which a society influences and determines the kind of mass media that it eventually winds up with. The tracing out of the historical development of the media in a given society, with proper attention to the social, cultural, economic, and political events which shaped their directions of growth at given times, provides a fruitful way to understand the media of that society as they exist at present and to forecast the probable directions which they are likely to take in the future. This can provide a framework for later comparisons between societies. Second, historical analyses of the media themselves within a given society *on a comparative basis between media* have not been widely reported. This has been attempted in the present volume within a sociological perspective. The media are cultural innovations; they spread through societies according to the same principles as other cultural innovations. Furthermore, they influence each other in that process. Adequate analyses of these societal and inter-media influences have not been widely available for students in communication courses. The first chapters of the present book were prepared to meet this need for my own students; I sincerely hope that they will prove useful for those of others.

The book tries once again to portray the process of human communication. Many other authors have tried their hand at this perplexing task. What the present analysis tries to do is to bring together the many ideas on this subject which have been advanced by writers from a variety of disciplines and points of view. The semanticists, symbolic interactionists, students of comparative animal behavior, mathematical model builders, and learning psychologists have all made important contributions to understanding human communication. The present analysis tries to present to the student a relatively simple perspective on such communication, one which also includes a place for *mass* communication.

Extensive effort has been made to analyze the background and theoretical sources of the *mass* as a major concept in the study of "mass" communication. Much of the earlier thinking about the media rested upon a particular interpretation of that term which may not be apparent to students of mass communication from disciplines other than sociology. The older theories which rested upon this concept are posed as a background and point of departure for more contemporary analyses. While those older theories themselves are of little substantive significance in explaining the media as they are now studied by communication researchers, they are still the basic orientation of the layman and the beginning student who may be looking at the mass media through a new conceptual framework provided by a course in mass communication.

In treating the more contemporary theories of mass communication, the present work does not attempt to summarize and report in great depth on the vast number of empirical studies of the "effects" of mass communication which have accumulated in the literature. This is not one of its basic purposes. Most instructors in communication courses make this a major part of their presentations. Also, excellent summaries already exist (such as those of Klapper or the more recent one of Larsen). For these reasons the present author saw little need to retrace this ground. This does not mean that the relevance and importance of empirical research is not fully appreciated. It is in fact the matrix out of which theoretical integration of the field of mass communication may one day be achieved. For present purposes, however, only those studies which played a more or less central role in the development of a particular theoretical statement are noted.

The discussion of the mass media as social systems is intended to explore the use of functional analysis as a conceptual tool for portraying the mass communication process in a systematic way. Functional analysis as used in the present work is more of a means of describing the media within a particular perspective than a theory as such. The validity of the asserted propositions which pose systematic relationships between the components of the system remain to be demonstrated empirically. In spite of this, it is heuristically useful in that it can give to the student an appreciation of the stability which is inherent in the complex set of human relationships that make up the mass media of communication operating within a particular society.

The present second edition, therefore, attempts to pull together a number of theoretical ideas—some widely studied already and some not well investigated—so as to give an organized indication of about where we are at present in the development of theories of mass communication. In aiming at this goal, the second edition does not differ in purpose from the earlier version. However, the second edition contains new material. For one thing, it brings up to date the charts and tables in Chapters II, III, and IV showing the continued growth and/ or decline of each of the several media. It provides revised interpretations of these trends. More important, it presents a completely rewritten version of Chapter VII, "Contemporary Theories of Mass Communication." In particular, it discusses a theoretical view of the role of the media in creating and sustaining cultural norms related to a variety of behaviors. This "cultural norms theory" is growing in significance in assessing media effects. This potential effect of the media, involving possible indirect influences on behavior through the creation of "definitions of the situation" for the individual, is under current empirical investigation and it underlies much contemporary criticism of the media. At the center of the controversy is the question of the role of the media—particularly television—in stimulating violence through the depiction of violence. In a society in which violence is becoming increasingly common, it may be natural to look to media portrayals of violence as a possible culprit. Because of their massive presence, the media are easy to blame for the disturbances in our cities and on our campuses. Before reaching hasty conclusions one way or the other, however, the issues need adequate theoretical formulation. Only then can relevant empirical research be designed and the significant issues identified. While no claim is made that the present formulation of the cultural norms theory provides the needed theoretical base, it presents at least a modest beginning. Overall, it remains clear that in seeking adequate theories of mass communication, linking the•media to societal and individual effects, much remains to be done.

The author would like to acknowledge the contributions of the many pioneers and contemporary students in this field from whom he has learned so much and from whose ideas he has freely drawn: Paul Lazarsfeld, Elihu Katz, Joseph Klapper, Bernard Berelson, Morris Janowitz, Herbert Blumer, Otto Larsen, Harold Lasswell, Carl Hovland, and Robert Merton are but a few. To the many researchers, essayists, and other writers from the many fields which have built up the body of information that has been accumulated to date, I express my respect. Finally, to my friend, the late George Lundberg, who persuaded me to write this book, I acknowledge a lasting intellectual debt.

Melvin L. De Fleur
1970

Chapter I

THE COMMUNICATION REVOLUTION

THE ORIGINS of human speech are lost in the mists of prehistory, but our most informed guesses suggest that man was a communicating animal, living in small bands nearly a million years ago, using simple tools and supporting some limited social organization. Languages developed slowly during the succeeding eons, with few fundamental innovations other than slow changes in general structure, grammatical complexity, and vocabulary size. During this period, communication was technologically limited to the range of the human voice and to the accuracy of the human memory. A single man might have spoken to a multitude, but only if the multitude had been collected together face-to-face in an acoustically favorable location. Aside from this, he could neither extend his ideas effectively across space, nor preserve them accurately through time.

Then, about 250 generations ago, man invented writing. To be more accurate, writing appears to have been developed independently in several areas of the world some centuries ago, not at a specific point in history but over an extended period of time. The early stylized picture writing of the Egyptians is roughly familiar to most of us. Technically, this is not the same as alphabetical writing. The cuneiform of the Mesopotamian area, which consisted of wedgelike impressions in clay tablets, made use of more conventionalized symbols as substitutes for sounds. The Chinese also invented writing of a somewhat different technical nature at a later date, as did the Mayas even later on the Yucatan Peninsula. For our purposes, the point of major significar

1

is that in the perspective of man's total existence and experience on this planet, writing is a relatively recent innovation.

Although in a strictly technical sense, a number of societies of the world could have been called literate within the past two thousand years (in the sense that a written language had been adopted or invented), this literacy certainly did not extend to the majority of the citizens of those societies. For the humble farmer, soldier, or village dweller, writing was a remote process which occurred at the courts of kings or within the centers of religion. The use of written symbols for reading and writing on the part of the common people has become widespread only during the last ten or fifteen decades. Even today, two-thirds of the way through the 20th century, with space travel becoming commonplace, the majority of mankind is still illiterate.

Mass literacy had to await the development of printing. When Johann Gutenberg slowly turned the handles of his crude wooden press to imprint with movable type the first copies of his famous Mazarin Bible, he could have had no thought that he was adding an important cultural element to the growing accumulation of technology in Western society, which would lead four centuries later to the emergence and flowering of mass communication.

With writing present in Western society, plus the new possibility of multiple reproduction of written documents, and with new political systems in the making that would give the common man increasingly responsible decision-making roles, the emergence of techniques of mass communication waited only widespread education and technological advances in the process of printing.

The basic idea of a newspaper had developed quite early in Europe, in England, and in the new United States. The American colonial press had been established for some years before the new nation was formed, distributing small papers and pamphlets to the educated elite. Their content was, as we shall see in more detail, at a level of sophistication and taste beyond the capacities of the common citizen. They did provide, however, the basic form around which to develop a new kind of newspaper aimed at the broad base of artisans, mechanics, and merchants who constituted the growing middle and working classes of the emerging urban-industrial society. When a means was found to finance a cheap paper for wide distribution, and the techniques were invented for rapid printing and distribution, the first true mass medium was born in the form of the penny press. As we will note more fully later, these events occurred in the mid-1830's in the city of New York. The mass newspaper was a great success and within a very few years it spread to many parts of the world. The third decade of the 19th century, then, saw the technology of rapid printing and the basic idea of a newspaper combined into the first true *mass* medium of communication.

Two points are important in these events. First, the mass newspaper, like the other media which followed it, was an invention that occurred only after a complex set of cultural elements had appeared and accumulated within the society. Second, like almost all inventions, it represented a combination of these elements in a social setting that permitted the acceptance and widespread adoption of the newspaper as a culture complex. As a technical device, it was consistent with, and perhaps even required by, other cultural institutions of the day. The relevant institutional structure of the society in terms of economic, political, and educational processes, as well as demographic and ecological patterns provided a setting within which the particular combination of elements represented by the penny press could emerge and flourish.

With the appearance and acceptance of the mass press, the pace of man's communicative activity began to increase sharply. By midcentury the telegraph became a reality. Although not a *mass* medium of communication, this device was again an important element in a technological accumulation that would eventually lead to mass electronic media. A few decades later, experiments were being carried out successfully that were prerequisite to motion pictures and to wireless telegraphy. With the dawn of the 20th century, Western society was about to experience the development of techniques of communication that had been beyond the wildest flights of imagination a century earlier. During the first decade of the new century, motion pictures became a form of family entertainment. This was soon followed in the 1920's by the development of household radio and in the 1940's by the beginnings of home television. By the early 1950's, radio had reached saturation penetration into American homes, with additional sets widely dispersed in automobiles. There was multiple penetration in the form of bedroom and kitchen radios, and a growing number of transistorized miniature sets. The late 1950's and early 1960's saw television beginning to approach such saturation. Mass communication had become one of the most significant and inescapable facts of modern life.

This brief sketch of the major milestones in the ability of man to communicate with his fellows indicates that the principal events of this historical process have occurred within the memories of substantial segments of the living American population. A society without radio and television was experienced by many of our present citizens, and for the older generation there were no neighborhood motion picture theaters to attend on Saturday night. Even the venerable newspaper is, as we have shown, only a dozen decades old. Most of the communication devices, which now play such an important part in our daily activities, have been with us but a brief moment if viewed within the extended span of man's social and cultural life. Little wonder we are not yet ready to make final pronouncements as to their impact on our society. These changes have come very easily and gently for the majority of us. They have been more than welcome as newspapers with interesting and easy reading or delightful boxes in our living rooms that entertain, amuse, and inform us. It may seem strange to suggest that these devices, which have invaded our homes, represent a kind of *communication revolution,* a set of rapid technological changes unique in the history of mankind. Each of these media has added to the total daily availability of language-using opportunities for the average citizen. Thus, the accumulation of these devices within recent history has implied a dramatic increase in the pace of communicative behavior for the majority of people in Western society; a fundamental change, the impact of which remains to be fully assessed.

The entrance of the newspaper, the radio receiver, or the television set into the home of the common man represents a technological change which has greater significance for the ordinary person than our largest accomplishments at the frontiers of science. With satellites and spacecraft streaking through space, we may lose sight of the fact that these achievements are remote from the routine daily activities of the majority of us. The television set, however, which has moved into our living rooms is a technological device which has an immediate and direct impact. The children of our society spend more than 20 hours a week, on the average, viewing its offerings. The television set and the other media at the very least are innovations around which the ordinary member of society organizes his life in different patterns because of their presence.

While social scientists have not reached a full understanding of the impact that these media are having upon the psychological, moral, economic, political, creative, cultural, or educational aspects of the ordinary individual's life, they have begun to accumulate a base of research findings which will increasingly aid in understanding these issues. The growth of the social sciences as disciplines employing quantitative procedures and the logic of science, like the development of the mass media themselves, has occurred principally within the last thirty years. Within that brief span, a limited number of sociologists, psychologists, and others have specialized in the dispassionate study of the role of the mass media within our society. As larger numbers of research specialists turn their attentions to this field, we may expect the generalizations growing out of such research to yield more complete understanding of the relationship between the mass media and the societies within which they operate. In large part, discussions as to that relationship have been carried on in the past within something other than a dispassionate and objective framework. As each of the major media of communication emerged in our society, it became the object of considerable controversy and debate. These debates began when the first issue of the penny press hit the streets of New York in 1834. They continue today with respect to the role of radio, paperbacks, television, comic books, magazines, and films in relation to a variety of issues.

One of the major tasks of sociologists or other students of mass communication in assessing this communication revolution, and the controversies which it has caused, is to accumulate scientific findings concerning the impact of the media on their audiences in order to replace emotional speculation with valid evidence as a basis for public discussion about mass communication. The different media have variously been charged with responsibility for (1) lowering the public's cultural tastes, (2) increasing rates of delinquency, (3) contributing to general moral deterioration, (4) lulling the masses into political superficiality, and (5) suppressing creativity. This is a damning list, and if the apparently innocent devices in our living rooms are actually guilty of such monstrous influences, they should of course be viewed with alarm. The problem is that spokesmen for opposite points of view tell us that our newspapers, radios, television sets, etc., are not insidious devices for evil, but are in fact our faithful servants or even saviors in that they are (1) exposing sin and corruption, (2) acting as guardians of precious free speech, (3) bringing at least some culture to millions for the first time, (4) providing harmless daily entertainment for the tired masses of the urban industrial labor force, (5) informing us of the world's events, and (6) making more bountiful our standard of living by their unrelenting insistence that we purchase and consume products to stimulate our economic institution. If such claims are true, to reject such benefactors or even to suggest that their content is uninspiring seems an act of flagrant ingratitude. Until reliable research findings can present a convincing case that the media either are or are not causally related to the claims of their critics or champions, these controversies will continue to rage.

A second task for the student of communication is to identify the basic nature of the communicative act. A general theory of human communication (mass or otherwise) remains to be worked out. Many promising leads are available from general semantics, social psychology, the study of learning, etc. As yet, however, no comprehensive theory has been advanced that incorporates the many isolated but well-validated propositions available from such disciplines into a systematic explanation of human communication in general. The place of mass communication within such a conceptual scheme, of course, will remain a continuing problem until such a theoretical framework has been developed.

Another of the major tasks for those who specialize in the scientific study of the media is to provide adequate data with which to evaluate the consequences of operating mass communication systems under varying conditions of ownership or control. That is, within differing political structures, economic systems, and historical-cultural settings, the structure of the mass media themselves can be expected to take different forms. The production, distribution, and consumption of mass media content is sharply influenced by questions such as whether or not the society is a free enterprise democracy, an outright totalitarian dictatorship, or something in between. Societies where mass communication systems operate under conditions of ownership and control quite different from those of the United States can provide a basis for comparative research. Similarly, studies of the historical development of particular media in particular societies offer possibilities of inducing generalizations about the way in which the various forms of the mass media have developed under different sociocultural conditions.

The sociological assessment of the communication revolution, then, centers around three broad but fundamental questions:

(1) What has been the impact of societies on their mass media? What have been the political, economic, or cultural conditions which have led them to operate in their present form?

(2) How does mass communication take place? Is mass communication a separate phenomenon from other types of communication? Does it differ in principle or only in detail from more direct interpersonal communication?

(3) What has been the impact of the mass media upon society? What influences have they had on the psychological processes, overt behaviors, or normative cultures of the people among whom they have flourished?

For several reasons, it is to the third question above that the majority of mass communication research has in the past been addressed. The first question, although of central sociological significance, has not captured much of the attention of research specialists and scholars. To some degree, the same is true of the second question. It appears likely, since the storm of criticism and controversy surrounding the media has been phrased largely in terms of the third of these fundamental questions, that sociologists and other communication researchers have been guided in their investigations less by theoretical significance than by the dictates of popular interest. Whatever the reasons for this lack of balance between these three issues, the first and second questions have received considerably less scholarly attention than the third. In several of the chapters which follow, special attention will be given to discussions of ways in which the social and cultural conditions in the United States have had a role in shaping our mass media. An attempt will also be made to pull together what we now know about the nature of the communicative act. In addition, considerable attention will be given to the third question.

What of the future? Can we assume that the final forms of mass communication have already been invented and adopted? If the past is even the crudest guide to the future, the answer must be an emphatic *no*. No industry seemed more secure and no medium seemed more ubiquitous than radio during the late 1930's and the 1940's. The same was true of the powerful motion picture industry. Before the advent of television, these two media appeared as unassailable. But when television diffused widely during the 1950's both of these older media experienced declining audiences and severe economic problems. In the decades to come, within our own lifetimes, the communication revolution should continue at an increasing pace. The sociological principle that a society's rate of invention increases geometrically as its technological culture base increases arithmetically indicates that our present television sets, transistorized portable radios, and superspectacular movies will soon seem as obsolete as the Model T Ford. While the exact forms of the new media to come cannot be predicted, the conclusion that they will inevitably arrive seems inescapable.

Chapter II

SOCIETY AND THE MASS PRESS

THE FIRST of the basic questions posed for analysis in the previous chapter is the most logical starting point for sociological assessment of the communications revolution. We may begin, then, by asking what has been the impact of the American society as a social and cultural system on the development of its mass media of communication? The mass media as they exist today in our particular society have a somewhat unique structure of control, a particular set of institutionalized norms relating them to their audiences and readers, and characteristic forms of content. They have worked out specific types of financial support and clearly defined relationships to other important social institutions such as government. They have all experienced in greater or lesser degree a somewhat repetitive set of problems associated with conflicts between their goals and the goals, aspirations, and hopes of those whose cultural tastes and educational backgrounds are substantially higher than those of the common citizen. Finally, their developmental patterns, in terms of their quantitative spread as innovations through the society and in terms of general problems encountered during their institutionalization as culture complexes, have been rather similar from one medium to another.

Each of the media was, from the point of view of the ordinary family, a new device that could be adopted or rejected as a form of technology within the home or at least as an innovation requiring the family to adopt new modes of behavior. The sociological principles governing the adoption of innovation by individuals and families are becoming increasingly understood. While the mass media today are intimately involved in the stimulation of innovative behavior, they can also be viewed as innovations themselves. A study of their adoption patterns as well as the social and cultural variables related to their spread can reveal some of the ways in which a society can significantly influence and shape its mass media.

We need not go far back in history to talk about a society without mass media. For more than half a century after the original thirteen colonies had declared their independence from England, there was no true mass press to bring news to the average person. There were limited circulation newspapers to be sure, but these tended to differ sharply in their content, cost, audience, method of distribution, and size of circulation from the later mass readership papers (which came in the third decade of the 19th century). Motion pictures and broadcasting (both radio and television) have long technical histories; but as devices playing a part in the communications behavior of the average family, they are innovations of the present century.

A full understanding of how our various media came into being at the particular times they did requires considerably more than a mere listing of inventions of technical apparatus along with a few dates and names. The historical study of the mass media within any societal context, for the purpose of establishing recurrent patterns which have appeared during their growth, requires that attention be focused upon the three important questions: (1) What technological elements or other cultural traits accumulated in what pattern to be combined into new culture complexes such as the mass newspaper, film, radio, or television industry? (2) What were the social and cultural conditions of the society within which this accumulation took place and how did these conditions create a climate favorable for the emergence and widespread adoption of the innovation? (3) What have been the patterns of diffusion of the innovations through the society, and what sociological conditions have been related to their rates and patterns of growth?

Obviously, all complex questions of this kind cannot adequately be answered within two or three chapters of one small book. Such issues require the extended attention of investigators with different perspectives from the various social sciences and scholars devoted to the study of each particular communication medium as well. Our task, then, will be to sketch briefly the highlights of these historical developments in an attempt to illustrate, within the context of the American society, the impact a society can have in shaping its mass media. We will summarize very briefly some of the major events and social forces that have been associated with the development of each of the larger media of communication within the United States. Beginning with the press, newspapers, motion pictures, radio, and television will be discussed within the framework of the three questions noted above.

THE MASS PRESS

The basic culture traits that were later to be combined into a mass newspaper extend far back into history. The modern newspaper is a combination of elements from many societies and from many periods of time. Even before the birth of Christ the Romans posted newssheets called *acta diurna* in public places. The Chinese and Koreans were using movable type and paper for printing several centuries before these appeared in Europe. In the 16th century, well after printing had come to Europe, the Venetian government printed a small newssheet which could be purchased for a *gazeta* (a small coin). The use of the word "gazette" to refer to newspapers has survived to this day. Something closer to our modern idea of a newspaper appeared in the early 1600's in Germany. Scholars of the history of journalism suggest that many of the features of the modern newspaper, such as the editorial, sports articles, illustrations, political columns, and even comics were used in one place or another long before the true mass press came into being.

Printing was introduced to England in the late 1400's, but it was not until 1621, nearly a century and a half later, that early forerunners of the newspaper began to appear. These were called *corantos*. Their content focused on foreign intelligence, and they were not published regularly as was the case with actual newspapers that came later. From the beginning, the publication of corantos was strongly regulated by the government. The 17th century in general was one of close regulation, or attempted close regulation, of all forms of printing. One of the interesting patterns discernible in the history of the press is that in societies with strong central governments, an unregulated press tended to grow only very slowly. In areas where centralized authority was weak, the press tended to develop under less control and to advance more rapidly. In a general way the greater the extent to which a form of government is actually dependent upon favorable public opinion, the more likely it is to support a free press. Where the common man plays significant roles in the determination of his own political destiny, the distribution of news and political opinions is an important process.

Strong monarchies, or societies with other forms of highly centralized power, do not require active public discussion of issues about which every citizen must reach an informed decision.

The long struggle to establish the important principle of freedom of the press was fought during a period when the older feudal monarchies were beginning to decline, and new concepts of political democracy were on the rise. Such considerations immediately suggest that one of the most significant changes in Western society, favoring the development of some form of mass communication, was the changing political institution that eventually vested voting power in the majority of citizens. This long and complex change established traditions of journalism which from the very beginning made the newspaper an arena of public debate, partisan protest, and political comment. By the time the other major media emerged, this political transformation had been substantially achieved and neither motion pictures nor the broadcast media, in the United States at least, have developed the deep interest in politics that has long characterized the press. These variables and factors have obviously been related in different patterns in other countries.

During the period before the seeds of the American and French revolutions began germinating, the whole fabric of Western society was undergoing change. The Dark Ages had given way to the Renaissance, and the ancient feudal society with its rigid stratification pattern was slowly being replaced by a new social structure within which a strong middle class would be a key element. These changes were inseparable from the growth of commercialism that eventually culminated in the industrial revolution itself. This commercialism was to be dependent upon improvement in the availability of various kinds of communication media. Techniques were sorely needed to coordinate manufacturing, shipping, production of raw materials, financial transactions, and the exploitation of markets.

Rapid, long-distance media would be slow in coming. Meanwhile, the rising middle class itself began to constitute an *audience,* not only for the latest information about commercial transactions, but also for political expression, essays, and popular literary fare. In England, these needs were met by such skilled writers and journalists as Addison, Steele, Samuel Johnson, and Daniel Defoe. In the American colonies a middle class with commercial interests developed rapidly. New England was a land of ships, seaports, and trade of all kinds. During the first part of the 18th century a number of small newspapers were published. Many were financial failures, but some survived over a period of years. Their circulations were never large, usually well under a thousand. By the time the Declaration of Independence was written, there were about thirty-five of these small and crudely printed newspapers in the thirteen colonies. For the most part, their publishers eked out a precarious existence by selling their newspapers on a subscription basis (they were relatively expensive) and by carrying a few commercial announcements. If the publisher happened to be a postmaster, or could land a government printing contract to help out, the financial risk was not so great.

The colonial press, as these papers are collectively called, was edited and published by men who were not great literary figures with the exception of notable American colonial journalists such as the remarkable Benjamin Franklin. They were still using basically the same printing technology that had been used by Gutenberg three centuries earlier. They did not have a mass audience with widespread reading skills. There were few large concentrated urban centers that could serve as markets, and they lacked an adequate basis upon which to finance a mass press. However, a complex array of culture traits had accumulated in the society, including elementary printing technology, private ownership of newspapers, and, as was mentioned, the principle of freedom of the press.

Before a true mass press could develop, a series of sweeping social changes was necessary in Western society. The changing political roles of the common citizen have already been mentioned. Also noted was the growth of commercialism, which led to changing patterns of social stratification and the rise of the middle class. To these can be added the necessary development of printing and paper technology, which increased its tempo with the mechanical advances of the early industrial revolution. Finally, when mass public education became a reality with the establishment of the first statewide public school system (in Massachusetts) during the 1830's, the stage was set for a combination of these many elements into a newspaper for the common man.

A number of printers and publishers had experimented with the idea of a cheap newspaper that could be sold not by yearly subscription but by the single copy to the urban masses. Various approaches to this problem were tried both in England and in the United States, but without success. It remained for an obscure New York printer, Benjamin H. Day, to find a successful formula. His little paper, the *New York Sun,* began modestly enough on September 3, 1833, with the motto "It Shines for ALL." As subsequent events proved, it did indeed shine for all. Day had begun a new era in journalism that within a few years would revolutionize newspaper publishing.

The *Sun* emphasized local news, human interest stories, and even sensational reports of shocking events. For example, to add spice to the content, Day hired a reporter who wrote articles in a humorous style concerning the cases brought daily before the local police court. This titillating content found a ready audience among the newly literate working classes. It also found many critics among more traditional people in the city. The paper was sold in single copies for a penny in the streets by enterprising newsboys. These boys soon established regular routes of customers; and circulation rose to 2000 in only 2 months. The breezy style and vigorous promotion of the paper shot this figure up to 5000 in 4 months and to 8000 in 6 months. The astonishing success of this controversial paper had the rest of the newspaper publishers in an uproar. By this time the steam engine had been coupled to the new rotary press. The famous Hoe cylinder press was available in the United States, along with abundant supplies of cheap wood pulp newsprint. The technical problems of producing and distributing huge numbers of newspapers on a daily basis had largely been solved, and the emergence of the mass press was an accomplished fact.

The *Sun* attracted its impressive circulation primarily by appealing to new readers who had not previously been reached by a newspaper. One of the most important features of Day's penny paper, and of those which followed it, was the redefinition of "news" to fit the tastes, interests, and reading skills of this less educated level of society. Up to that time, "news" generally meant reports on social or political events of genuine importance, or of other happenings that were of widespread significance. Benjamin Day, however, filled his paper with news of another sort—accounts of crimes, stories of sin, catastrophe, and disaster—news the man in the street found exciting, entertaining, or amusing. His staff even invented an elaborate hoax, concerning new "scientific discoveries" of life on the moon. When the hoax was exposed by another paper, his readers took it in good humor because it had been fun to read about. The paper was vulgar, cheap, and sensational; it was aimed directly at the newly literate working masses who were beginning to participate in the spreading industrial revolution. There was some serious material in the paper to be sure, but its editorials and reports of political and economic complexities were much more superficial than in the earlier partisan papers written for more politically sophisticated readers. By 1837, the *Sun* was distributing 30,000 copies daily, more than the combined total of all New York daily papers when the penny paper was first brought out.

Imitators of Day had started rival papers almost immediately. The penny press was a financial success because it had great appeal for advertisers. In fact advertising revenues were its only real support; the penny for which it was sold could scarcely pay for the raw newsprint. But goods and services for mass consumption could be successfully advertised through the penny press. These advertisements reached huge numbers of potential customers much more successfully than those appearing in the preceding limited circulation newspapers. Patent medicines, "for man and beast," were one such mass-use product that played a prominent part in supporting the new penny papers. Early department stores also took readily to the newspaper as a means for publicizing their wares.

For such advertisers, size of circulation was thought to be a good index of the amount of profit one could anticipate. The newspaper that could place an advertising message before tens of thousands attracted the advertising dollar. This simple principle set into motion rugged competition between rival papers for new readers. This had important implications for the development of the popular press during the latter half of the 19th century, and indeed had implications for mass media that would not even be invented until a full century later! The foundations of an important institutionalized pattern of social relationships, which linked advertiser, media operators, and audience into a functional system for the production of particular types of mass communicated content, were worked out in the early years of the development of the mass press.

Meanwhile, Benjamin Day's most colorful and successful competitor was James Gordon Bennett, who founded a newspaper empire on only 500 dollars in a barren office in a cellar. Bennett, a shrewd and tough Scot, started the *Herald* in New York. He flouted the conservative moral norms of the time and published flaming news accounts of murder trials, rape, sin, and depravity. At the same time, he reported effectively on politics, financial matters, and even on the social affairs of high society. This variety of content gave his *Herald* a wide appeal and made it a strong financial success. Bennett himself made many enemies with his forceful and often scandalous newspaper articles. For example, in 1836 he wrote:

. . . Books have had their day—the theatres have had their day—the temple of religion has had its day. A newspaper can be made to take the lead in all of these in the great movements of human thought and of human civilization. A newspaper can send more souls to Heaven, and save more from Hell, than all the churches or chapels in New York—besides making money at the same time.[1]

Although Bennett's startling prediction did not come true, the newspaper was about to begin its spread through the American society and to start playing an increasingly important part in its daily affairs.

THE PERIOD OF RAPID DIFFUSION

Although the mass newspaper arrived in the 1830's, it was still limited in terms of news gathering, printing technology, and distribution. Before it could diffuse widely into the homes of every American city, a number of important problems remained to be solved. The decades just preceding the Civil War were filled with important mechanical, scientific, and technical developments that were to make it possible for the infant mass newspaper to grow into a giant. Railroads were built between the principal cities in the eastern part of the nation. The steamboat arrived as a major transportation link after about 1840. The telegraph grew increasingly useful as a means for rapid transmission of news from the scenes of important events to editorial offices. These developments substantially increased the newspaper's appeal to its readers and increased the number of people to whom newspapers could be distributed.

More and more, newspapers began to seek out the news. The role of reporter grew more complex and specialized as papers added foreign correspondents and special news gatherers of various kinds. Reporters were sent to the scenes of battles; others were permanently stationed in Washington, D.C. to cover political events. The "surveillance" function of the press became well established.[2]

The rising demand for fresh news was met by newly formed cooperative news-gathering agencies, which made use of the telegraph wires. These agencies sent stories to papers in many parts of the country with which they had contractual arrangements. Through such agreements, the staff of a paper near an event could cover the story for many papers elsewhere, thereby greatly reducing the cost of news gathering. These advances brought the newspaper to the smaller cities and towns and even to the newly established cities in the West.

Printing technology was making rapid strides, moving toward ever-increasing automation. Revolving presses, with print cast in a solid lead stereotype, became capable of rolling out ten and even twenty thousand sheets an hour.

The Civil War brought maturity of a sort to the newspaper as it reinforced the concept that the paper's principal function is to gather, edit, and report the news. The older concept of the paper as primarily an organ of partisan political opinion had faded considerably. The post-Civil War papers increasingly clarified their roles as locators, assemblers, and purveyors of the news. This is not to suggest that newspapers became either uninterested or nonpartisan with respect to politics—quite the opposite. Individual editors and publishers often used their newspapers to champion causes of one kind or another and to wage "crusades" against political opponents. But at the same time, they were all heavily involved in straightforward reporting of the news.

Papers continued to gain in popularity. In 1850 there were about two copies of a daily newspaper purchased in the United States for every ten families. The rate of growth of newspaper circulations increased steadily, but not spectacularly, until the 1880's. During the two decades 1890–1910, however, the rate of newspaper circulation per household rose sharply. This rapid growth actually continued until about the time of World War I, and then tended to level off during the 1920's. But, the last decade of the 19th century is one of special significance in the growth of the press, because it was the beginning of a new kind of journalism. While this new journalism did not become permanently established, it left its mark upon the American newspaper. Let us look in greater detail at this development because it is of importance for understanding patterns in the development of later mass media as well.

YELLOW JOURNALISM

While the newspaper was growing up, the second half of the 19th century was for American society a period of rapid change, upheaval, and transition. It was an era characterized simultaneously by an expanding frontier, a devastating Civil War and its aftermath, the arrival of wave after wave of immigrants, a pronounced rural to urban movement, and an increasingly rapid transition to an industrial society. Any one of these changes could have fundamentally altered the basic social organization of the society. Their combined effect was even more deeply felt. New norms replaced old; firmly established mores were cast aside; a traditional way of life gave way to a new type of social order. If ever a society was in a state of cultural upheaval and transition, it was American society during the five decade period of the last half of the 19th century.

This was the social context within which the mass press spread and matured. Against this background of cultural conflict and *anomie*, the new medium had to devise and institutionalize the basic codes that would regulate its responsibilities to the public which it served, and would place limits upon the kind of content it contained. With the normative structure of the society itself in a state of turmoil, it is not surprising that the mass press was able to work out its "canons of journalism" only after a rather stormy period of adolescence.

One of the most dramatic episodes in the development of the press was the period of "yellow journalism." By the 1880's, the newspaper had achieved wide adoption by American households, and further astronomical increases in circulation were increasingly difficult to stimulate. At the same time, the press was firmly established financially as long as the number of newspapers sold could be kept at a maximum. Within this competitive context, brutal struggles for additional readers developed between the leaders of giant rival papers. In New York, in particular, William Randolph Hearst and Joseph Pulitzer fought by any means available to expand their circulation figures. These were, of course, the key to increased advertising revenues and profits. Various features, devices, "gimmicks," styles, and experiments were tried by each side to make its paper more appealing to the mass of readers. Newspapers today contain many of these devices, which were actually products of the rivalries of the 1890's. (One of these was color comics. An early comic character was called the "Yellow Kid," from which "yellow journalism" is said to derive its name.)

As the competition intensified into open conflict, the papers turned more and more to any sensationalistic device that would attract additional readers, no matter how shallow and blatant. In the early 1890's yellow journalism burst full blown upon the American public:

... the yellow journalists ... choked up the news channels upon which the common man depended, with a callous disregard for journalistic ethics and responsibility. Theirs was a shrieking, gaudy, sensation-loving, devil-may-care kind of journalism which lured the reader by any possible means. It seized upon the techniques of writing, illustrating and printing which were the prides of the new journalism and turned them to perverted uses. It made the high drama of life a cheap melodrama, and it twisted the facts of each day into whatever form seemed best suited to produce sales for the howling newsboy. Worst of all, instead of giving its readers effective leadership, it offered a palliative of sin, sex and violence.[3]

Yellow journalism offended a sufficient number of groups and individuals so that a storm of criticism gradually made clear to the operators of the mass press that they had exceeded the limits which the society, and particularly representatives of the norm-bearing institutions, would tolerate. Intellectuals in general and the literati in particular were deeply wounded. The great new means of communication, which held forth the tantalizing potential of mass cultural and moral uplift, had in their eyes turned out to be a monstrous influence for societal degeneration.

Leaders in religion, education, law, and government increasingly voiced strong protests. The press lords were faced with the threat of losing public confidence, and the even more chilling possibility of regulation imposed from without. These considerations led a number of major publishers to begin to put their own houses in order. Gradually, the press became less sensational and more responsible. A set of codes and norms defining its limits and responsibilities gradually became increasingly clear. Professional associations of editors and publishers established canons of journalism intended to guide their members. While the mass press today varies substantially in its degree of adherence to such codes, the excesses of yellow journalism appear to be a thing of the past. Out of these experiences of the newspaper came a number of institutionalized principles which in one way or another have helped clarify the roles, responsibilities, and policies of media that followed. The way in which this has been the case will be made clear in later sections.

Quantitative Diffusion Pattern of the Mass Press

Data on newspaper circulations are given in Table 1. These figures report both circulations of newspapers and the growth of the number of households for the period 1850–1967. Rates of newspaper circulation *per household* are given in the last column of the table. The pattern which these rates form over time is shown in Figure 1. Rates of daily newspaper circulation per household follow an S-shaped "curve of diffusion" that is more or less typical of growth patterns followed by a variety of cultural innovations as these are adopted by a given population.[4] This particular innovation had been accepted by only a small proportion of the population up to about 1870. A number of factors (e.g., limited education, transportation, and printing facilities) played a part in keeping the number of "early adopters" small. Between 1880 and 1890, however, the newspaper swept rapidly through the American population to a point of near saturation by the end of the century. Improved press technology, better transportation, and spreading literacy were significant factors in this sudden change. By 1910, at the eve of World War I, there was more than one newspaper circulated for every household. Thus, during the first decade of the century, newspapers were becoming what anthropologists call a cultural universal in the American society.

Increases in circulation slowed after 1910. The apparent high point in the American newspaper occurred in about 1920, just following World War I. Since that time, the medium has suffered a steady and very noticeable decline. Even further improvements in the technology of newsgathering, printing, distribution, and literacy have not slowed this downward trend. Even though more newspapers are sold today in an absolute sense, they have not kept pace with increases in the number of American households.

But what has been the basis of this decline? An adequate theory of the relationship between a society and its mass media should be able to account for such a social change as well as for media growth. In other words, an analysis of the invention, adoption, and institutionalization of a cultural item such as the newspaper, and the organizational complex which produces it, would be incomplete without consideration of variables that can lead to its *obsolescence*. As far as the newspaper is concerned, the factors that have led to its decline are not difficult to suggest. Other media forms, meeting needs in the population similar to those met by newspapers, began to appear in the society during the 1920's. Radio developed as a household medium during that decade. Shortly afterward (during the 1930's) weekly news magazines began to gain mass acceptance. Even the film played a part. By the late 1940's and during the 1950's, of course, television swept through the American society. To a greater or lesser extent, each of these *functional alternatives* to the newspaper has eaten into the circulation of the daily press. Each, in some sense or other, provides news, information, or entertainment in a way that once was the exclusive province of the newspaper.

But what of the newspaper's future? It will probably survive with some further decline. At present, few breakthroughs in newspaper technology are likely. Few changes in literacy or other factors related to potential increases in readership are probable in the immediate future. By the same token, there will probably be few radical innovations among the newspaper's competitors, at least for some time.

TABLE 1

THE GROWTH OF DAILY NEWSPAPERS IN THE UNITED STATES
(1850–1967)

Year	Total Circulation of Daily Newspapers (Excluding Sunday)	Total Number of Households	Circulation Per Household
1850	758,000	3,598,240	.21
1860	1,478,000	5,210,934	.28
1870	2,602,000	7,579,363	.34
1880	3,566,000	9,945,916	.36
1890	8,387,000	12,690,152	.66
1900	15,102,000	15,992,000	.94
1904	19,633,000	17,521,000	1.12
1909	24,212,000	19,734,000	1.23
1914	28,777,000	22,110,000	1.30
1919	33,029,000	23,873,000	1.38
1920	27,790,656	24,467,000	1.13
1925	33,739,369	27,540,000	1.22
1930	39,589,172	29,997,000	1.32
1935	38,155,540	31,892,000	1.20
1940	41,131,611	35,153,000	1.17
1945	48,384,188	37,503,000	1.29
1950	53,829,072	43,554,000	1.23
1955	56,147,359	47,788,000	1.17
1960	58,881,746	52,799,000	1.12
1961	59,261,464	53,464,000	1.11
1962	59,848,688	54,652,000	1.10
1963	58,905,000	55,189,000	1.07
1964	60,412,000	55,996,000	1.08
1965	60,358,000	57,251,000	1.05
1966	61,397,000	58,092,000	1.06
1967	61,561,000	58,845,000	1.05

SOURCES: U.S. Bureau of Census, *Historical Statistics of the United States, Colonial Times to 1957* (Washington, D.C., 1960), Series R 176, p. 500; Series R 169, p. 500; Series 255, p. 16; Series A 242–244.

U.S. Bureau of Census, *Historical Statistics of the United States, Continuation to 1962 and Revisions* (Washington, D.C., 1965), Series R 170, p. 69.

U.S. Bureau of Census, *Statistical Abstract of the United States* (Washington, D.C., 1968), Table 747, p. 507.

U.S. Bureau of Census, *Current Population Reports: Population Characteristics,* Series P 20, No. 166 (August 4, 1967), p. 4.

NOTE: All figures after 1960 include Alaska and Hawaii.

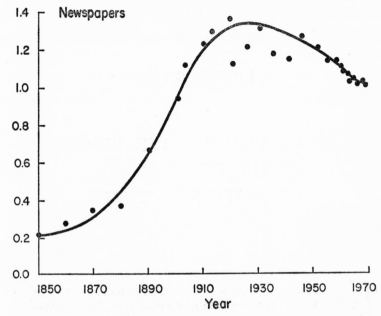

FIGURE 1. The Cumulative Diffusion Curve for Daily Newspapers; Subscriptions Per Household in the United States (1850–1970)

Also, research on the kinds of satisfactions and gratifications provided for readers by the daily newspaper indicates that it is deeply woven into the daily lives of ordinary people. It provides certain unique services and gratifications. When the newspaper does not come, it is sorely missed. It apparently plays a role in our communication system that alternatives are unlikely to displace, at least for the present.[5] Thus, while newer media, and possibly others to come, pose a challenge to the newspaper, it remains as an institutionalized culture complex and as one of our fundamental modes of mass communication.

Our brief look at the newspaper has indicated in broad outline the accumulation of technological elements and other traits that were combined to form the early mass press. It has also indicated a number of social and cultural conditions that helped shape its financial basis, its relationship to our political institution, and the variables that help determine its content. Finally, we have provided a sociological perspective on the way in which the daily newspaper was adopted as a cultural innovation, as well as the prospects for its survival as part of the American system of mass communication.

Chapter III

SOCIOCULTURAL INFLUENCES
ON THE DEVELOPMENT
OF MOTION PICTURES

THE HISTORICAL antecedents of the motion picture extend backward
in time at least as far as those of the mass press. The development
of its technological base, however, followed quite different paths and
was a result of quite different social forces than those which characterized the background of the newspaper. The technological culture traits
that were eventually combined in the development of the projected motion picture were invented and refined as by-products of several somewhat unrelated developments in science. The major contributors to the
fundamental technology upon which motion pictures depend were for
the most part men of science who made their discoveries or developed
their apparatus while searching for solutions to specific scientific problems. There were exceptions of course, but generally the men who
were to become the fathers of the motion picture had little interest in
the development of a medium by which people could be entertained.
They were far more interested in discovering such things as the physical
principles of light refraction, the neurological basis of human vision, or
the way in which the illusion of motion was perceived. Throughout
this long history of invention and development there were also indications of great potential popular interest in a medium of entertainment
based upon the projection of shadow images. At least, the nonscientific
friends of many of the inventors were continuously fascinated by the
strange devices and effects these men produced.

THE INSTITUTIONAL FRAMEWORK

We may contrast sharply the development of the motion picture, as it occurred within the institutional framework of science, with that of the newspaper, which was traced out in rough outline in the previous chapter. We saw that the history of the mass press was very closely related to important developments within the *economic* and *political* institutions of Western society. Commercialism and political partisanship were characteristics clearly associated with early forms of newspapers as well as the more mature press. When a viable financial structure was found for a mass press in the democratic capitalistic societies, this structure was based firmly upon commercial advertising. And, even though the newspaper redefined its relationship to political affairs more than once, the press continued to regard political activities as one of its major areas of responsibility, at least in reporting and analyzing if not in actual proselytizing. The motion picture, on the other hand, has never been more than marginally related to the presentation of commercial advertising content in a direct sense. And, although movies occasionally deal with politically or socially significant themes, they have not often been used (in American society at least) for the open advocacy of political ideologies. A complete understanding of the impact of society upon its communication media requires that we understand why, in the United States, motion pictures became a major communication medium devoted principally to entertainment rather than edification or persuasion, and why paid admissions as opposed to advertising or government subsidy provided their most important means of financial support. The present discussion cannot fully provide answers to these questions. It can show, however, within the context of American society, how political, social, and economic forces played a role in the formation of the motion picture as a system of mass communication. Comparative analyses of other societies, where the structure of the political institution and the functioning of the economic system have followed different patterns, would indicate why the form and content of the entire system of motion pictures varies from country to country.

THE ACCUMULATION OF TECHNOLOGY

The early history of the motion picture is more accurately the story of developments related to three scientific-technical problems that required solution before an apparatus for the projection of motion pictures could even be envisioned. We need to consider these three problems, and some of the technical devices that eventually led to their solution. The story of these devices and solutions is, however, inseparable from that of the men who achieved them, but the accomplishments of these men are intimately related to the social and cultural context within which they achieved their success.

The first of the major problems referred to above was the development of a means for showing shadow images with the use of an *illuminated projector* that passed light through a transparency to cast an image on a reflecting screen in a darkened room.

The list of elements making up this complex is obviously extensive. Basic to the technology of such projection is some understanding of the principles of optics. The use of mirrors and lenses is involved, including concave mirrors for the focusing of light from an artificial source so as to pass through a lens in suitable intensity. Of these various traits, the lens is probably the oldest. Adequate records exist showing that by the time of the Greeks, the "burning glass" was known by men of science.[1] Archimedes (born 287 B.C.), for example, attempted to construct a large lens, which was purported to have the power to set a ship on fire some distance away by focusing the rays of the sun. Whether this was actually accomplished or not is debatable, but the principle was understood. The field of optics was advanced further by the work of the Arab philosopher and scientist Alhazen (born A.D. 965) who worked out some of the first explanations of refraction and reflection with mirrors and lenses. The pace in invention and cultural accumulation was agonizingly slow in this beginning period. By the time of Roger Bacon (born 1214), scientists and philosophers had done little more than discover various ways to use mirrors in periscope-like devices to reflect images in such ways that the ordinary folk of the time were mystified.

One of the more important elements from this early period of invention and discovery was the *camera obscura* (literally "dark room"). The basic idea is that of the pinhole camera, within which a weak, upside-down, and reversed image of an external scene can be observed on a wall opposite a small hole in a lightproof rectangular chamber.[2] This phenomenon had undoubtedly been observed very early in man's experience, but the rules and principles of its operation were not systematically investigated until the time of Leonardo da Vinci (born 1452).[3] Leonardo worked in small room sealed from light and into which light rays coming from a scene outside were allowed to enter through a hole about the size of a pencil. The image formed on the opposite wall could be clearly recognized as the outside scene in full color, although weak and sometimes blurred. With the suitable addition of a lens for focusing and a mirror to reverse the image, the camera obscura became a useful device for artists who were concerned with problems of perspective and color in the painting of landscapes. The camera obscura caught the attention of a number of scientists as well as artists, and it was used to observe eclipses of the sun. This avoided the damage to the eyes that resulted from direct observation, even through darkened glass.

The camera obscura fell into the hands of magicians, charlatans, and others who preyed upon the ignorance of people of the period and who claimed magical powers for themselves on the basis of the effects they were able to produce. Scientists and experimenters were constantly harassed with the problem of magic and witchcraft being associated with their work. Attempts were made from time to time to publicize the "secrets" of these wonders to dispel such charges. This was true not only in the area of optics, but in all branches of science. One of the most interesting of the early attempts to popularize science was a book by Giambattista della Porta or Giovanni Battista della Porta (born about 1535). In the seventeenth "book" (chapter) of his famous work, *Natural Magick,* translated and published in English in 1658, della Porta discoursed on the matter "Of Strange Glasses" (lenses and mirrors).[4] After discussing the mechanics of the camera obscura, he went on to describe how the device could be used to present plays and other amusements:

How in a Chamber you may see Hunting, Battles of Enemies, and other delusions.

... nothing can be more pleasant for great men, and Scholars, and ingenious persons to behold; That in a dark Chamber by white sheets objected, one may see as clearly and perspicuously, as if they were before his eyes, Huntings, Banquets, Armies of Enemies, Plays and all things else that one desireth. Let there be over against that chamber, where you desire to represent these things, some spacious Plain, where the Sun can freely shine: Upon that you shall set Trees in Order, also Woods, Mountains, Rivers, and Animals that are really so, or are made by Art, of Wood, or some other matter. You must frame little children in them, as we use to bring them in when Comedies are Acted: and you must counterfeit Stags, Bores, Rhinocerets, Elephants, Lions, and what other creatures you please: Then by degrees they must appear, as coming out of their dens, upon the Plain: The Hunter he must come with his hunting Pole, Nets, Arrows, and other necessaries, that may represent hunting: Let there be Horns, Cornets, Trumpets sounded: those that are in the Chamber shall see Trees, Animals, Hunters Faces, and all the rest so plainly that they cannot tell whether they be true or delusions: Swords drawn will glitter at the hole, that they will make people almost afraid. I have often shewed this kind of Spectacle to my friends, who much admired it, and took pleasure to see such a deceit.[5]

Although della Porta was a scientist, it is clear he had a talent for showmanship. He also had considerable interest in using various devices and effects to astonish his friends. The moving images of the camera obscura were a source of delight and amusement for the wealthy and prominent of Europe for some time to come. All through the historical development of the technological devices which were prerequisites to the modern motion picture, we see the continuous fascination and awe with which the projected image was regarded by the nonscientist.

The camera obscura, of course, produced its image from light reflected from objects in bright sunlight. A step of some importance lay in substituting artificial light for the sun and in passing this light through a transparency instead of depending upon reflected light. The illuminated projector that could throw images on a screen, using precisely the principles involved in the modern slide projector, became a reality through the work of Athanasius Kircher (born 1601).[6] Kircher was a German Jesuit whose learning and scientific discoveries earned him a place at the Collegio Romano, where with the encouragement of Pope Urban VIII, and other ecclesiastical authorities, he pursued mathematical and scientific investigations. Kircher was able to demonstrate in a dramatic showing before a distinguished audience the crude projector which he developed and the dim images it produced with the use of hand-painted transparent slides. Kircher became the object of ugly accusations and gossip as a result of his work. He was accused of being in league with the devil and of practicing the black art of necromancy (conjuring up the spirits of the dead for nefarious purposes). The principles upon which his ghostlike projected images were called forth were not well understood, or were deliberately misunderstood by his enemies, even among the most highly educated men of the time.

Kircher went on to refine his apparatus. He, too, was something of a showman and he arranged ways in which stories could be told, illustrated with projected slide images. A number of later inventors added refinements to the "magic lantern" and still others, more directly interested in showmanship, exploited its use as a means for entertainment. The solution to the first basic technical problem of the motion picture was thus complete by about 1645.

The second of the major problems requiring solution was to discover the way in which the human being perceived the *illusion of continuous motion*. Unlike the problem of the projector, this involved a relatively large number of elements. Complex discoveries in the theory of human vision and human perception had to be worked out. Essentially, the problem was to discover how a rapid series of drawings, or other figures, could be presented to the human eye in such a way that the afterimages and the visual lag occurring within the neural-perceptual processes would cause the figures to be consciously experienced as a single figure in smooth motion.

In the early 1800's children in London and Paris were playing with a device called the Thaumatrope. It was a small disc about the diameter of a teacup mounted on a shaft. It had a figure on the front and another on the reverse side. By twirling the device with the aid of short strings or threads various illusions could be created. Several forms of the toy were prepared with amusing figures of one kind or another. There has been some controversy about the origin of this device, but it is generally attributed to a London physician, Dr. John Paris (born 1785). It was described and discussed by David Brewster, the student of the polarization of light and the inventor of the kaleidoscope, in one of his scientific works. The toy is not of particular significance in itself except insofar as it depended upon the phenomenon of visual lag and suggested that an illusion of motion might be produced by rapid presentation of slightly changed figures in sequence.

One of the great students of the so-called persistence of vision or visual lag was the Belgian scientist Joseph Plateau (born 1801).[7] Early in his career, he became interested in various aspects of vision and particularly the way in which the human being perceives motion and color.

Plateau's doctoral thesis from the University of Liege outlined the problems of vision that had to be considered in producing the illusion of motion in the human perceiver. First, each individual figure, drawing, or picture in a rapidly presented series had to remain stationary for a brief but sufficient amount of time for the neural-perceptual processes to apprehend it clearly. The eye does not operate absolutely instantaneously. It takes a certain amount of exposure time for a given scene to register an impression. The rapidly whirling blade of a fan seems to "disappear" because of this feature of the human eye. The second point is also a time factor. An impression once registered within the neural-perceptive mechanisms of vision does not stop registering at the instantaneous moment the stimulus itself is withdrawn. There is a substantial lag as the impression lingers briefly. The simplest demonstration of this principle can be made with a common "sparkler" such as children use on the Fourth of July. If this bright light is moved quickly in a figure eight pattern in the dark, the individual "sees" a complete figure eight, and not simply a rapidly moving dot of light. This is what is meant by visual lag.

With these principles in mind, Plateau worked out a rather cumbersome apparatus of belts, cranks, pulleys, disks, and shutters that enabled him to create a simple illusion of movement, based upon the rapid successive presentation of a drawing. He refined this to a large disk, around whose circumference was arranged a *series* of drawings, each of which was slightly varied so that the same basic figure advanced to a slightly different position from one drawing to the next. When suitably shown to a subject a moving figure was perceived. This machine was called the Phenakistiscope or Fantascope. It was the first true motion picture device. A system had thus been invented, based upon known principles of vision, that permitted a human observer to perceive an illusion of smooth and continuous motion from serially presented still figures. Professor Plateau pursued his quest for the principles of vision to the point where he experimented on himself by testing the effect of prolonged staring at the most powerful light he could think of—the sun. As a result of such experimentation, he became permanently and tragically blind, and much of his important work had to be done after his sight had gone completely. The irony of a blind scientist establishing the visual principles of the motion picture is paralleled only by the tragedy of the deaf Beethoven, who wrote some of the world's great symphonic music after his hearing totally failed, and Edison's invention of the phonograph when he himself was deaf. Joseph Plateau moved the accumulation of technology a great step closer to the day when the motion picture would be used as a cheap form of entertainment for the amusement of the masses.

Only the last of the three important technical problems needed to be solved before the culture complex of the motion picture as a form of mass communication could be synthesized out of these elements. The technology of *photography* in general, and of taking rapid sequence photographs of objects in motion in particular, remained as prerequisites to the motion picture.

The scientific struggle to achieve a workable photographic process is in itself a story of tremendous difficulties, great complexity, and deep fascination. It depended upon developments within the growing science of chemistry and in particular upon that part of the science concerned with chemical changes in substances produced by the action of light. The development of photography also involves the already familiar camera obscura. When sufficiently reduced in size, provided with a lens and a removable reflecting surface coated with a light sensitive chemical, it became the camera with which we today capture the inverted images of scenes reflected within. In so doing we are still utilizing principles known in the time of da Vinci. The problem, then, was not the camera itself, but the film. What chemical processes and techniques could be used in order to fix the image of the camera obscura? Even here knowledge was well advanced by the beginning of the 19th century. In the early 1700's it had been shown experimentally that there were particular chemical compounds, such as various salts of silver, that were rapidly altered by exposure to light. This realization permitted speculation about the possibility of capturing the image of the camera obscura. It was not until the third decade of the 19th century, however, that the mechanical and chemical techniques for preparing, exposing, developing, and fixing an actual picture from the camera obscura were worked out.

Solutions to this problem were in fact reached by at least three separate individuals. Each worked without knowledge of the other; each employed a somewhat different approach; and each announced his discoveries at almost the same time (between January and March of 1839). Louis Daguerre in France, William Talbot in England, and John Herschel also of England, all succeeded in producing photographs based upon the same general chemical principles, but upon rather different specific mechanical techniques.[8] The Daguerre process produced a sharp image of exquisite detail on a polished plate of copper that had been coated with silver metal and exposed to iodine fumes (to form silver iodide). Light striking this plate when correctly exposed in the camera caused the silver iodide to be drastically altered where bright light struck, but to remain relatively unaffected where light of less intensity fell on the plate. The resulting *daguerreotype* produced an excellent picture with sharpness and clarity. There were no negatives; only one picture could be obtained at a time. The processes of Talbot and of Herschel employed paper treated with similar light-sensitive chemicals and produced negatives, from which it was necessary to make a second (positive) print. Although the latter procedure proved in time to be by far the most useful, it was in its early form very crude, cumbersome, and unreliable. Furthermore, the pictures produced on the paper of the time lacked the precision of the daguerreotype. For this reason, the daguerreotype was an instant success, and the name of Louis Daguerre became very well known. In a world which had never seen a photograph, the daguerreotype seemed an almost incredible accomplishment. Such pictures were, in fact, when carefully produced, the equal of the finest and most carefully made photographs of today. The use of a polished metal plate of silver gave them a great brilliance and sharpness. They were less "grainy" and showed more detail than even a very good modern paper print. Some indication of the world's astonishment and delight with this new product of science can be gained from the following account, written in 1839 by the editor of a popular American magazine, who had just seen a display of the new daguerreotypes:

We have seen the views taken in Paris by the "Daguerreotype" and have no hesitation in avowing that they are the most remarkable objects of curiosity and admiration, in the arts, that we ever beheld. Their exquisite perfection almost transcends the bounds of sober belief. Let us endeavor to convey to the reader an impression of their character. Let him suppose himself standing in the middle of Broadway, with a looking glass held perpendicularly in his hand, in which is reflected the street, with all that therein is, for two or three miles, taking in the haziest distance. Then let him take the glass into the house, and find the impression of the entire view, in the softest light and shade, vividly retained upon its surface. This is the "Daguerreotype"! [9]

The acceptance of the Daguerre photographic process was immediate and enthusiastic. Improvements in technique were quickly made so that portraits were possible in indoor "salons." Rigid iron head clamps were used, and light was reflected from overhead skylights. The first daguerreotypes were made in the United States in 1839, the same year that the process was announced in Paris by various scientists and enthusiasts, among whom was Samuel F. B. Morse. While Morse is best remembered for his work with the telegraph, he was actually a portrait painter of some distinction. He was also a professor in the arts of design at the University of the City of New York. The daguerreotype was closely related to both these interests. He was immediately enthusiastic about the new art, and he actually visited Daguerre in France in 1839. Morse became an active daguerreotypist in New York, and is said to have supported himself financially by making portraits and by training students in the process, while awaiting recognition and financial support from the U.S. government for his telegraph.

The production of portraits provided an immediate link between the art of daguerreotypy and the art of making money. Here was a new kind of profession, requiring a relatively brief period of technical training, a small outlay for equipment, and the potential of financial success. The 1840's were in the United States a period of economic depression. A number of enterprising young men were looking about for an opportunity to enter into some venture whereby they could make a living without investing large capital and without having to undergo extensive university professional training. The occupational role of daguerreotypist was almost made to order. There were villages, towns, and cities all over the settled part of the United States that had not yet seen the new process. The cost of having one's portrait made, especially in the smaller sizes, was not prohibitively expensive. A family of average means could easily afford it. Daguerreotype equipment was loaded on wagons, flatboats, oxcarts, and mules. The photographer's art spread out over the country. In all the major cities, daguerreotype salons were established, and business was exceedingly brisk. Quality of work varied greatly. The roving daguerreotypist with poor training and little skill turned out a dreadful product, paying attention neither to graceful poses nor to technical precision in the production of the plates. Some combined the photographic art with other occupational pursuits. A given individual might be a combination blacksmith, cobbler, watch repairer, dentist, and daguerreotypist. It was possible to have one's boots resoled, watch oiled, teeth pulled, horse shod, and portrait made—all in a "package deal" and all at one stop, so to speak.[10]

At the other extreme were the beautiful and luxurious salons that developed in the principal population centers. Mathew Brady gained an international reputation as a fine portrait artist in Washington D.C., long before the beginning of the Civil War.[11] Stretched between these two extremes were establishments large and small that were producing over *three million portraits a year* in the 1850's! [12]

The insatiable demand for portraits was undoubtedly related to a number of characteristics of the times. The United States was a society on the move. People were no sooner settled on one frontier than another opened up farther on. The males often left their families in more settled areas until they could be brought out to reasonably favorable accommodations. The movements of population associated with the various gold rushes, land rushes, oil booms, and other events separated men from their wives, and sons from their parents. Along the Atlantic seaboard, the Yankees were a maritime people, with men folk often "gone awhaling" or engaged in world commerce and shipping. The vast upheaval and movement of persons during the Civil War gave portrait photographers a decisive boost. Portraits were a way of reducing the pain of the separations in some small measure. In some degree, they even breached the great gulf between the living and the dead. They were prized reminders of significant primary group ties.

The product of the portrait artist had also a deep tradition as a status symbol. To be able to display portrait paintings of assorted ancestors testified to a family's place in time. It was a society where aristocratic birth or family background were decreasingly related to power and wealth. Still, there was a pronounced cultural lag which permitted such symbols to suggest high social position. Achieved criteria were becoming objectively more and more important, but ascribed criteria had not lost their significance. In the early period of the industrial revolution, some members of the newly rich are even said to have hired portrait painters to manufacture for them a set of distinguished ancestors. For the less wealthy, and for the growing middle and working classes, the silver iodide plate of the daguerreotypist provided a mass consumption substitute for the more distinguished canvas of the portrait artist.

Some indication of the rapid adoption of this innovation can be gained by a study of the growth of the occupational classification "photographer." Table 2 indicates the number of photographers in the United States per 100,000 population for the years 1840 to 1900. These data show the rapid diffusion of photography as a cultural innovation. This occurred in the four decades 1850–1890. By the last decade of the 19th century, there is little doubt that the average American was widely familiar with photographs. The transition between a still photograph and one that gave the illusion of motion was not an impossible step for the imagination of the ordinary citizen.

The technology of photography became increasingly sophisticated; it also became more and more important as part of the growing industrial complexes of society. Factories for the manufacture of photographic chemicals, photographic equipment, and photographic plates were developed. Among these, the name of George Eastman is perhaps the most widely known. The first daguerreotype photography had given way to other techniques. The ambrotype grew in popularity and then quickly declined. The tintype was widely used during the Civil War, but was discontinued with the perfection of newer technology. Wet plate processes, with light-sensitive chemicals suspended in a thin

TABLE 2

THE GROWTH OF THE OCCUPATION OF PHOTOGRAPHER
IN THE UNITED STATES (1840–1930)

Year	Size of Population	Number of Photographers	Photographers per 100,000
1840	17,000,000	0	0
1850	23,000,000	938	4
1860	31,000,000	3,154	10
1870	39,000,000	7,558	19
1880	50,000,000	9,990	20
1890	63,000,000	20,040	32
1900	76,000,000	27,029	36
1910	92,000,000	31,775	35
1920	106,000,000	34,259	32
1930	123,000,000	39,529	32

SOURCE: U.S. Bureau of Census, *Population Census of the United States* (For the decennial years 1840, 50, . . . 1930, Washington, D.C.)

collodion film on glass, were widely used for many years. It was the dry plate, however, that permitted preparation in advance of glass photographic plates. This led to their commercial manufacture, distribution, and sale. The miniature camera and the amateur camera were popularized when this technology became available. George Eastman went into the business of manufacturing such photographic plates in the year 1880. From a modest enterprise started on a capital of three thousand dollars, he built a business that thirty-four years later could pay five million dollars for exclusive rights to the patented process of making flexible photographic plates on nitrocellulose film.

The development of flexible film actually occurred in several places at the same time.[13] One type of film was developed in France in the early 1880's. One of Eastman's chemists applied for a patent in the United States at about the same time. Still another patent was applied for in 1889, by the Reverend Hannibal Goodwin, an obscure clergyman. These films were all based upon more or less the same process, with minor variations from one to the other. However, several years of extremely complex litigation ensued, during which the patent office reviewed and re-reviewed the various claims. The patent was finally awarded to Goodwin, but in the meantime, Eastman had been manufacturing flexible film for almost a decade. This roll film was designed for his "foolproof" camera that could be used by the novice (the famous Kodak). With the availability of this flexible film, the development of the motion picture was a step nearer. Edison had produced the light bulb, and the technology of electricity was widely understood. The study of objects in motion had progressed with the use of instantaneous still photography. As we have seen, the principle of projection had long been common knowledge. The neurophysiology of visual lag had been worked out to an adequate extent. It remained only for these various elements to be combined into a workable projected motion picture. The camera obscura and the magic lantern were about to be combined in ways that would have astonished Kircher, della Porta, and da Vinci.

It was Thomas Alva Edison who achieved this combination, but hundreds of others in various parts of the world also contributed.[14] From Edison's laboratory came the motion picture camera, and a motion picture projector. It was early in the last decade of the 19th century.

Edison lacked confidence in the financial feasibility of the commercial projection of motion pictures on the ground they would be a novelty and the public would soon lose interest. His conception of the way to exploit his device commercially was to develop a machine that could be used by only one person at a time, paying a fee to view a few moments of photographed motion. His peep show Kinetoscope was scheduled for premiere at the Chicago World's Fair of 1893, but it was not ready in time. It was in fact the following year in 1894 when the Kinetoscope was placed on public exhibition for the first time. An enterprising exhibitor opened up a "Kinetoscope Parlor" with ten of the machines right on Broadway in New York. But the limitations of the Kinetoscope were severe, and the possibilities for a more complete exploitation of the magic lantern of movement were seen by a number of people both in the United States and in Europe. While Edison made the most significant contribution to the actual emergence of the motion picture by achieving the basic technological combination, it remained for more adventurous souls to try to perfect the technique and to turn it into a process for the mass entertainment of the multitude.

In the final years of the century, literally dozens of people were clamoring for patents in as many countries. They were looking for financial backing and for recognition of a variety of motion picture cameras or motion picture projectors. From England, France, Germany, and the United States came conflicting claims and reports that these devices had been invented, improved, modified, or perfected. It was in fact a period of high excitement, intense activity, and inventive ferment. Showmen such as Emile Reynaud in Paris were exhibiting projected moving picture stories, based upon the principle of animated drawings, with great success. It took no vast stretch of imagination to see that the commercial exhibiting of projected motion pictures could be a considerable financial success.

In 1895 an establishment was opened in Paris, called the Cinematographe. For a single franc a patron was admitted to a "salon" where he could view a few very brief films. The exhibition became so popular within a few days that it attracted thousands of viewers, and was operated on a standing room only basis.

The Cinematographe was soon exhibited in New York, and the system was widely imitated. In the meantime, in England, the motion picture camera was focused on such events as the Derby of 1896, and the exhibition of these projected films caused a sensation. These and other attempts at public showings stimulated further interest in the idea of projected motion pictures for entertainment of the public. It was clear that there were fortunes to be made in the motion picture business.

By this time, Edison had become convinced. He combined efforts with a young American inventor named Thomas Armat, who had obtained certain patents involved in the improvement of the projector. Together they manufactured the Vitascope, or Armat-Edison projector, which was used in the most successful of the early efforts to exhibit motion pictures to the public.

With the dawn of the 20th century, then, all of the technological problems had been solved. The motion picture theater had been more than two thousand years in the making, but it was now ready to take its place as the second of the major mass media of communication and to play its role in the growing communication revolution.

THE EARLY MOTION PICTURES; CONTENT AND AUDIENCE

From the outset, motion pictures were concerned with content in low cultural taste and intellectual level. Even the very first moving pictures in the Edison Kinetoscope parlors exhibited such inspiring works as *Fatima and her Danse du Ventre,* which was the sensation of the Chicago World's Fair in 1896. Naïve and slapstick comics were popular. A view of a mischevous boy squirting a hose on a dignified dowager or open pornography (within the limits of the era) such as

the brief *How Bridget Served the Salad Undressed,* were received with
enthusiasm by the patrons of the penny arcades in which the Kine-
toscopes were installed.[15] These first films, with their boxing matches,
low comedy, and shimmy dancers, can be contrasted with the efforts
of the first printers. Gutenberg's first product represented the most
significant and important ideas of his time. Books in the early period
were works of philosophy, science, art, or politics. The motion picture
concerned itself in its early period with the trivial and inconsequential.
The content mattered little to anyone; it was the novelty of movement
that was the important factor. The film's first audiences stared with
open mouths at any picture that moved. But even among the habitués
of the penny arcades, an important principle quickly began to manifest itself. Such films as *Beavers at Play* or *The Surf at Dover* brought
in fewer pennies than the brief but exciting *Danse du Ventre,* or the
titillating *What the Bootblack Saw.* Efforts toward the filming of more
serious or artistic subjects were not received with enthusiasm. Film
content aimed at more elementary gratifications was what brought in
the money. From the first, then, systematic relationships between audience tastes and the financial structure of the infant "industry" governed the production of film content. Audiences were selective in what
they would pay to see, and producers were selective in what they produced for profit.

It would be tempting to analyze the characteristics of the clientele
of the penny arcades, which were to say the least not located in the
more discriminating sections of the urban centers, and to draw the
inference that it was their low level of cultural taste that left a permanent stamp of mediocrity upon the film. The problem was that the
film moved out of the penny arcade very quickly, but it did not noticeably rise in the seriousness or in the artistic taste of its content. The
film went from the arcade to the vaudeville house, where it was exhibited as a scientific novelty following the major acts. Again, the
tastes of the burlesque theater governed the content of the films.

In about the year 1900, a number of enterprising arcade owners,
former circus operators, medicine showmen, ex-pitchmen, barkers, etc.,
began to rent unused stores, to equip them cheaply with benches or
chairs, and to project films with secondhand equipment. Their working capital was meagre, their repertoire atrocious, their establishment
dismal, but above all it was cheap. For only a nickel the audience
member could watch an assortment of exciting short pictures, ranging
from *Life of An American Fireman* to *Dream of a Rarebit Fiend.*
These were either trick movies of brief length or exciting little se-

quences of dramatic events such as the firemen responding to a call. Various names were popular, but the name "nickelodeon" caught on as a popular way of referring to these enterprises. The most important thing about them was that they were popular with people at the bottom of the social structure, and they made money. A few nickelodeons cleaned up their interiors, dressed up outside, and opened up in other principal cities in the country. The first decade of the 20th century, then, saw a new form of communication begin to spread. It was to become a true mass medium.[16]

The content of the films soon changed markedly. They became longer and more sophisticated technically. They did not rise far in taste or seriousness. Such fare as *The Great Train Robbery* was just about what the nickelodeon audience wanted to see in 1903. Films with stories became the norm in a very short time. These places of entertainment thrived in their most prosperous form in the same areas of the metropolis where the penny arcades were located. As the motion picture was establishing itself, its audience tended to be heavily weighted with poor immigrants, drifters, and the anonymous residents of the city's zones of transition. The most significant groups in numbers were by far the immigrants. The first ten years of the 1900's was a period of unprecedented immigration, unequalled in more contemporary times. Ethnic groups of various kinds were pouring into the United States from eastern and southern Europe. By the millions they established ethnic neighborhoods within the ecological and social structure of the city. Immigration laws were not strict by today's standards, and many of these new citizens were illiterate, even in their own language. A large proportion had no knowledge of English whatsoever. Substantial numbers were agricultural peasants in their own land. For these humble people, surrounded by a bewildering and complex industrial society which they had not yet begun to understand, the primitive movie was a source of solace and entertainment. The plots were simple; the stylized acting needed no knowledge of the language in order to understand the idea. Today's viewer is amused at the stereotyped facial expressions and the gross body movements of the actors in early films. Such techniques become more understandable when it is realized that the audience had only occasional subtitles with which to follow the plot in a verbal sense. Even many of the English speaking members of the audience could read only with difficulty, if at all, and a great many of the foreign-born knew not a word.

The immigrant, then, and his rustic counterpart newly arrived in the big city were the most important audience types toward whom the early nickelodeon movies were aimed. With slapstick and burlesque they even poked fun at such people themselves and made them laugh at their own plight. The country bumpkin and the immigrant were often seen in the films. The cop, the crook, the pretty girl, the jealous husband, the boss—this was about the total range of personalities that appeared in the movies. It was enough. Their antics were easily understood. In intensified form, such stereotyping and slapstick led to such content as the Keystone Cops and the pie-throwing scenes.

By the second decade, however, the nickelodeon had spread far beyond the urban centers. It had started to become a form of family entertainment. Enthusiastic operators were demanding more complicated fare. Movie companies had mushroomed to fill the demand for films. This booming entertainment medium was well on its way. The "star" system came; movies discovered the classics; more flexible techniques of photography were developed. The films grew longer to the feature length we are now accustomed to. This increase in technical competence was due in part to the growing enthusiasm of motion picture audiences. The dreary nickelodeons had given way by the beginning of the 1920's to much larger and more elaborate picture palaces. Some were so luxuriously decorated they almost appeared to be temples of worship for the new gods and goddesses of the screen. Such stars were receiving the adoration of millions of shop girls and factory hands. They were also receiving astronomical salaries which made Hollywood synonymous with ostentatious consumption of wealth.

The Great War had given the American film industry an unprecedented boost. The production of motion pictures in the studios of Europe had ceased after 1914, but the demand for films had become tremendous and world-wide. This placed U.S. films in the export market with an advantage, which was retained for years. The silent film, with written subtitles easily changed to any language, was made by directors and producers who were themselves immigrants from other countries. It was a particularly flexible product for export to foreign countries. Almost inexhaustible markets were opened up when the more remote regions of the world began showing films with subtitles in Urdu, Hindi, Chinese, Arabic, or whatever local language was required. If the local audience was not literate in its own language, a "storyteller" was employed to explain to the native audience what was transpiring in the film as it progressed. Any relationship between these versions and the original intent of the film's designers was purely coincidental. The political position of the United States in World War I, then, had the most significant impact upon the American motion picture as a mass medium. It made the medium one of world significance.

The events of the Great War also point up other ways in which a society can have an impact upon its media. When the war broke out in Europe, the American public increasingly began to focus its public opinions in two opposite directions. The pacifists wanted to stay out of the European war and to avoid engaging in any military expansion that might eventually lead the country into participation in the war. Those in favor of preparedness felt that the United States would more than likely have to enter the war at some point, and it might as well make military preparations to make the task easier if the need arose. These were issues of great importance during the years just before the United States declared war on Germany. When war came a large bloc of the American public still retained attitudes, opinions, and sentiments unsuitable for total commitment and participation in the war effort. To reduce these unhealthy pacifist feelings, George Creel, chief of the Committee on Public Information (the official U.S. agency for domestic propaganda), mobilized motion pictures as part of an all out effort to "sell the war to the American public." This thrust upon motion pictures a propaganda role which they had not played before, at least in the United States.[17] Motion pictures had been simply a form of entertainment. They had not seriously engaged in persuasion for political partisanship, moral uplift, social responsibility, or cultural betterment. In general, they had *followed* public tastes and attitudes, rather than *led* them. The somewhat limited experiences of the war, however, opened up new possibilities and objectives for the film as a medium of persuasion in the minds of some. Actually, the motion picture in its form as a medium of entertainment has never become a consistent vehicle for effective political or social comment. While Hollywood has cooperated during wartime and has occasionally produced a film with a social "message," these are considered departures from the norm. The position of the film in this respect is distinct from that of the newspaper, which has consistently assumed that it has the responsibility to instruct us politically.

During the last part of the 1920's the sound track came to the film. By this time the motion picture theater was a permanently established and respectable place of entertainment for American families. As a business the production, distribution, and exhibition of motion pictures was firmly entrenched in the American economy, and as a cultural innovation it had become deeply institutionalized into our weekly routines. Accurate records of motion picture attendance are available on

TABLE 3

THE GROWTH OF MOTION PICTURE ATTENDANCE
IN THE UNITED STATES (1922–1965)

Year	Average Weekly Movie Attendance	Total Number of Households	Weekly Attendance Per Household
1922	40,000,000	25,687,000	1.56
1924	46,000,000	26,941,000	1.71
1926	50,000,000	28,101,000	1.78
1928	65,000,000	29,124,000	2.23
1930	90,000,000	29,997,000	3.00
1932	60,000,000	30,439,000	1.97
1934	70,000,000	31,306,000	2.24
1936	88,000,000	32,454,000	2.71
1938	85,000,000	33,683,000	2.52
1940	80,000,000	35,153,000	2.28
1942	85,000,000	36,445,000	2.33
1944	85,000,000	37,115,000	2.29
1946	90,000,000	38,370,000	2.35
1948	90,000,000	40,532,000	2.22
1950	60,000,000	43,554,000	1.38
1951	54,000,000	44,656,000	1.21
1952	51,000,000	45,504,000	1.12
1953	46,000,000	46,334,000	.99
1954	49,000,000	46,893,000	1.04
1955	46,000,000	47,788,000	.96
1956	47,000,000	48,902,000	.96
1957	45,000,000	49,673,000	.91
1958	40,000,000	50,474,000	.79
1959	42,000,000	51,435,000	.82
1960	40,000,000	52,772,000	.76
1961	42,000,000	53,197,000	.79
1962	43,000,000	54,369,000	.79
1963	44,000,000	55,705,000	.79
1965	44,000,000	56,956,000	.77

SOURCES: U.S. Bureau of Census, *Historical Statistics of the United States, Colonial Times to 1957* (Washington, D.C., 1960), Series H 522, p. 225 and Series A 242–244, p. 15.

U.S. Bureau of Census, *Historical Statistics of the United States, Continuation to 1962 and Revisions* (Washington, D.C., 1965), Series H 522, p. 35.

U.S. Bureau of Census, *Statistical Abstract of the United States* (Washington, D.C., 1968), Tables 11 and 302, pp. 12 and 208.

U.S. Bureau of Census, *Current Population Reports: Population Characteristics*, Series P-20, No. 166 (August 24, 1967), p. 1 and p. 4.

NOTE: Figures do not include Alaska and Hawaii. Data on attendance for 1964 not reliably reported in sources. Household data from 1951 to 1961 revised for consistency with contemporary estimates of total population.

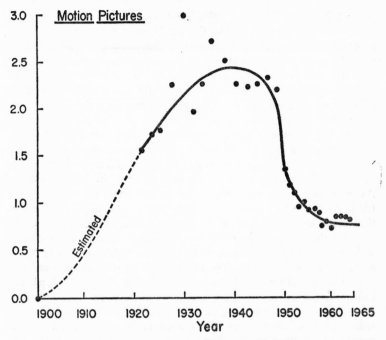

FIGURE 2. The Cumulative Diffusion Curve for Motion Pictures; Average Weekly Attendance Per Household in the United States (1900–1965)

a national basis beginning with 1922. By that time, the film was so popular that the number of paid admissions in an average week in the United States already exceeded forty million!

The adoption of the motion picture as a cultural innovation for mass use was both swift and extensive. The United States was literally transformed into a nation of moviegoers between 1900 and 1930. Table 3 shows both average weekly attendance from 1922 to 1965 and the number of households during the same period. Although attendance data are not available from 1900 to 1921, it appears most likely that this early period of the movies followed the estimated trend as shown in Figure 2.

Perhaps the most significant aspect of the adoption pattern for the film is its *variability*. This is particularly apparent in the middle section of the curve, when attendance figures fluctuated wildly. These were the Depression years; hard times in the early thirties had a sharp impact on moviegoing. Admissions dropped by more than 30 percent between 1930 and 1933. However, the late 1930's and the decade of the 1940's were the Golden Years for the film. Even so, functional alternatives were becoming increasingly available. As these grew in number and popularity, their impact on motion-picture attendance was to be little short of disastrous. Clearly, the rapid rise of television, beginning at the end of the 1940's and continuing through the next decade, had the deepest possible impact on the mass use of the motion picture. Even though the society as a whole was moving toward unprecedented economic affluence, average weekly attendance per household dropped from 2.35 in 1946 to only .96 in 1955. This drop has continued, although the rate of decline has slowed noticeably.

The movie industry struggled mightily to slow the rate of decline. As competition with television increased, numerous experiments were tried. At one point, moviegoers were issued special glasses so that they could see the picture in three dimensions. Screens widened—to almost unbelievable proportions in some cases. Special sound effects, with speakers in various parts of the theater, were tried. These "gimmicks" did not help much; the decline continued. Perhaps more significantly, the older moral standards governing film content all but collapsed. At an earlier time, motion pictures shown to American audiences were about as racy as the proverbial Sunday School picnic. Solid, middle-class America didn't need to be titillated with taboo themes to get them to pay at the box office. Today, unless a movie promises a bloodbath or frank sex portrayals, it may not be a big money-maker. Much legal maneuvering and litigation has accompanied this change, and the issues of "freedom of speech" versus "obscenity" have been widely discussed in connection with motion picture portrayals. Currently, public officials and others are sharply criticizing film violence.

Whatever the eventual significance of these issues within the context of the motion picture, it seems reasonably clear that the real pressure for change has been an economic one. Without their present appeal to the more elementary gratifications, movies might have disappeared as a major medium of mass communication. In fact, in spite of the present leveling trend of the curve, motion pictures have already lost more than *two-thirds* of the per capita business that they enjoyed in 1930. The most logical projection for the future would be that the decline will continue, and that the movie theater as we now know it will eventually disappear. This does not mean that films will no longer be made. Television provides an insatiable demand for even the dullest films—as any viewer of the Late Late Show will testify. Thus, while the industry may survive, or even prosper, the behavioral forms of its consumers appear likely to continue their present trend. The strong shift of interest of the American public from the movie screen downtown to the television screen at home is likely to continue as color television achieves saturation, and as TV moves toward codes concerning content which will probably eventually resemble those of contemporary movies.

The conditions and factors which are related to the abandonment of a given behavioral form within a social system have largely been neglected in the recent surge of interest in the innovation process. Obsolescence is a natural counterpart of innovation, and a necessary feature of an adequate theory of social change. There are undoubtedly systematic principles which govern the way in which a given item, trait, or culture complex is abandoned by a population. We no longer make much use of quill pens, detachable collars, automobile cranks, the Townsend Plan, and the chaperoned party for young adults. These forms undoubtedly followed some reverse pattern of declining usage, symmetrical in form to the usual S-curve of adoption. In spite of the obvious significance of such obsolescence patterns for understanding social and cultural change, no systematic theory is available concerning the conditions under which they are generated.

In the case of the motion picture, the causes of obsolescence are not particularly obscure. The Depression, the population shift to the suburbs, and, of course, the continued growth of the electronic media, have cut deeply into paid attendance. To these fairly obvious factors could be added the increasing congestion of central business districts where most theaters are located and the burden of mounting labor costs, which has resulted in continuous box-office increases and a correspondingly smaller number of consumers.

Overall, our analysis has shown the long and complex accumulation of culture traits and technological innovations that were necessary conditions for the emergence of the film as a medium of mass communication. It has indicated the many social and cultural conditions, such as wars, population shifts, and changes in the economic institution that were significantly related to the eventual widespread adoption and probable impending obsolescence of motion pictures as a behavioral innovation on the part of the American population.

The impact of a society on a communication medium could not be more clear than in the case of the motion picture. As a technology, and as an industry, it will undoubtedly continue to occupy a place in our social system. However, there are considerable doubts concerning its survival in the form in which it was originally adopted by our population.

Chapter IV

THE SOCIAL CONTEXT
OF THE BROADCAST MEDIA

IN TRACING the principal ways in which society has influenced the broadcast media, there are three somewhat distinct issues which require clarification. First, there are the numerous and complex social factors that established the need and consequent search for an instantaneous medium of communication that could leap across oceans and span continents. Second, there is the chain of scientific and technical achievements that accumulated as one invention led to another when various means of fulfilling the need were sought. Finally, there are the events that resulted in the translation of commercial wireless-telegraphy and radio-telephone technology into a mass medium with which to broadcast programs to the home receivers of entire nations. We might add, of course, the growth of television out of radio as still another issue; but as will be made clear, the newer medium not only shared a common history with radio but it inherited its financial basis, traditions, structure of control, and even much of its talent.

THE NEED FOR RAPID COMMUNICATION

Man's need for a reliable means of communicating rapidly over long distances increased relentlessly as his society grew in complexity. As long as his social activities were confined to a small band, which moved about together or stayed close to a fixed village, the range of the human voice, or at most the distance a strong runner could cover without rest, proved sufficient as a means for handling his communication problems. But as complex social organizations were invented for military, commercial, and governmental purposes, such groups were continuously faced with the problem of coordinating their activities without a really reliable method of transmitting information quickly over long distances.

Human ingenuity is vast, and men of every age have shown a remarkable ability to take the technology of their time and apply it in some fresh way to the solution of practical problems. So it was with long-distance communication. Our earliest records tell of military commanders who signaled information at night from the tops of hills with the use of torches arranged in previously agreed upon patterns or crude codes.

The word *telegraph* itself comes from the Greeks fully 300 years before Christ. Its two component words imply "at a distance" and "to write." In the Greek, Persian, and Roman civilizations social organization in military affairs, government, and commerce had far outstripped communication technology, and the inability to coordinate complex activities was a frequent source of great difficulty. Armies were defeated, navies were sunk, governments collapsed, and fortunes were lost (literally) all for the want of a word.

But an impressive array of technical gadgets were invented and pressed into service over the intervening centuries to find a solution to this cultural lag. Even primitive man, needing to communicate but sorely handicapped by his crude technology, was able to burn out the inside of a log and stretch the skin of an animal over one end to form a drum. With this he could conquer surprising distances using coded sounds. Smoke signals are another familiar example; carrier pigeons are still another (used right up into the 20th century). Flashing mirrors, lantern signals, cannon shots, and fire beacons were all used in the struggle to surmount distance and time. But these early communication techniques were severely limited. Most were terribly cumbersome and distressingly unreliable. Many depended upon good weather, and the others could handle only very simple messages.

In more recent times, many interesting communication systems were invented. All were in some way dependent upon line-of-sight vision between communicator and receiver. However, by relaying a message along a series of stations, complex messages could be sent over surprisingly long distances. During the height of Napoleon's power in France, that country actually had a total of 224 semaphore stations which spanned over a thousand miles in all.[1] This type of system was the most elaborate and widely used of all of the line-of-sight communication devices. An outgrowth of a simple idea developed by three French schoolboys for sending messages to each other, it depended upon positioning a pair of large wooden arms on top of a tower in such a way that given configurations represented the letters of the alphabet in agreed-upon patterns. The signals could be read and interpreted by a receiving operator in another tower several miles away. He in turn sent the message along to the next station, etc. It was expensive and cumbersome, but the system was in use in a number of European countries right up to the time that the electrical telegraph replaced it. The semaphore still has some limited applications, especially aboard naval vessels maintaining radio silence.

As Western society came into the 19th century, the need for a means of communication that would quickly transverse even the oceans themselves began to become critical. The tempo of commercial intercourse between nations had increased greatly with the advent of the industrial revolution. Great Britain was developing a colonial empire so vast and far-flung that it would be able to boast with impunity that it was one upon which the sun never set. Britannia ruled not only the waves but a substantial portion of the world's land surface and a sizable segment of the world's population. Other nations were also building mighty navies and great merchant fleets. They were consolidating new political systems, developing colonial markets, and exploiting new sources of raw materials. Along with all of this came fundamental changes in the very organizational nature of Western society. These changes have been discussed by social scientists in various terms such as complex organic evolution analogies, the movement from Gemeinschaft to Gesellschaft, the change from mechanical to organic solidarity, and the trend from a sacred to a secular society (to mention only a few). There can be little doubt that a communication medium such as the electrical telegraph was sorely needed in the face of growing societal complexity and could have been put to immediate, practical, and important use long before it was finally available.

The dream of an instantaneous telegraph based upon magnetic principles had been around in one form or another for a long time. Giovanni della Porta, the author of *Natural Magick,* had discussed a very special kind of lodestone (a type of iron ore with magnetic properties).[2] If two similar compasses were to be fashioned by using this mineral to magnetize their needles, it was said they would be locked together by some mysterious force so that if the needle of one were forced to point in a given direction, the other would then instantly and automatically move to the same orientation, regardless of intervening space.

With an alphabet fixed around the circumference of the compass, the telegraphic possibilities which such a system might provide were obvious. But sadly, search as they might, scientists, philosophers, and learned men were never able to find quite the right variety of lodestone needed to construct such a marvelous *sympathetic telegraph*. Like the philosopher's stone, the Golden Fleece, and the fountain of youth, it remained forever beyond their grasp.

THE BASIC THEORY OF ELECTRICITY

But while the legendary lodestone failed to provide the means for a telegraph, the scientific laboratory eventually would yield devices that would transcend the hopes and dreams of all of the ancient wise men. The development of an adequate understanding of electricity came during the 19th century as part of the great surge of accomplishment in the physical sciences. Radio itself was a by-product of a long, continuous, and basic inquiry into the nature of electrical energy.

The theorizing and research that led to this communication medium occupied the lifetimes of large numbers of scientific workers, only a few of whom ever achieved popular recognition, financial success, or even lasting scientific honors. The list of problems these men solved is simply staggering. Today's teen-ager who tunes in to his favorite program of popular music while lying on the beach and the factory worker who props up his feet at night and views his favorite ball team in action are acting out behavior systems that are the end products of centuries of brilliant scientific advances, the solution of which absorbed some of the most creative imaginations and most tireless workers of the last two centuries. These pioneers grappled with an endless list of conceptual, theoretical, and mechanical-technical problems whose solutions permitted today's systems of broadcasting.

The problems needing solution before radio could become a reality included the basic theory of electricity and elementary circuitry, including generating, conducting, and measuring electric currents. Also included were the theories of electromagnetic fields, coils, and the electromagnetic radiation and detection of high frequency oscillations. Another series of problems centered around the alteration of currents, such as rectification and amplification. The diode and triode electron tubes were required to couple voice transmission to the dot-and-dash wireless telegraph. Finally, for television, an offspring of radio, the problems associated with broadcasting patterns of light and shadow and receiving these on a viewing screen had to be solved. The light-sensitive photoelectron tube in the heart of the television camera was a substantial advance, as was the kinescope receiving picture tube. The latter two opened the way for commercial television.

The principles by which sound or light are converted to electromagnetic waves that can be broadcast through space, to be received and converted back into sound or light, involve the most basic of the physical sciences. Some of these principles govern the nature of matter itself.

The key to radio transmission and reception and to television is the *electron.* In oversimplified terms, the electron is conceptualized by physicists as an infinitesimally small *particle* that has the electrical characteristic of being negatively charged. Electrons, of course, are one major type of particle that make up *atoms,* but there are other kinds such as protons and related types that constitute the *nucleus* of a given atom. These tiny nuclear particles have positive electric charges that exactly match the negative electrical charges of the atom's electrons. It is this balance of electrical forces that holds the particles together in a given atom.

Each atom of the elements has a different number of electrons and other particles, making up its overall structure. The heavier a given element is, the more electrons it has in its atoms, and vice versa. An atom of a given element is a tightly organized structure of particles that are electrically balanced against each other in a tiny system. Some elements, however, have atoms whose outer electrons for various reasons are less solidly attached to their structures.

For some elements (like copper and many other metals) electrons can be temporarily picked off or added to the outer parts of these systems by chemical or electromagnetic processes, thus throwing the atom into a temporary electrical imbalance. When this happens, the atom attracts an electron from its neighbor to replace the one lost. Or if it has too many it passes one on to its neighbor. Then the neighbor reacts similarly with *its* neighbor, and so on. If the element is a good "conductor" of electricity, and is arranged in a long thin wire, the result will be a "flow of electrical current" along that wire. Nothing really "flows" of course, but the successive electrical imbalances in the atoms of the wires making up an electrical circuit can be thought of in this way. Storage batteries, generators, fuel cells, and many other devices are capable of producing these electrical imbalances at the end of a wire. This disequilibrium creates an energy source in the form of an electrical charge at the other end. From this comes our familiar host of applications of the resulting energy. It is used to create magnetic fields, heat, light, and other effects such as radio and television. If the foregoing seems complex, it is an indication to the reader of the difficulties that were overcome as part of the accumulation of ideas and technology prior to the invention of radio.

THE DEVELOPMENT OF ELECTRICAL TECHNOLOGY

All during the period from the Greeks up to the latter part of the 18th century, experimenters had marveled at the phenomenon of electricity. Static electricity was easily produced by friction, and with that principle in mind, experimenters built larger and larger devices for generating charges. The Greeks rubbed an amber rod on a piece of cloth and generated weak electrostatic induction currents capable of attracting a light pith ball suspended on the end of a thread. Centuries later, European scientists of the 1700's had elaborated the mechanics of this process to a point where they could generate awesome charges of static electricity with ponderous friction machines. Huge rotating disks with cloth pads to pick up the electrical charges were constructed. They astounded their friends by letting these charges smash between two metal points in lightning-like fashion up to a distance of several feet. Such machines were capable of attracting bits of thread or other objects from as much as thirty feet away. But actually, they were still using the same principle that had fascinated the Greeks, and they really did not understand why it all worked! While they must have been having a great deal of fun with their dramatic devices, they had not been able to solve the critical problem of *storing* electricity so that it could be used when and where it was needed.

Several people seem to have found a crude solution to this problem at about the same time. A jar half filled with water and corked with a wire down through the middle of the cork, can "store" a charge of electricity. One end of the wire must dip into the water and the other end must be temporarily attached to the business end of a friction machine that is generating static electricity. An unsuspecting soul who later grasps the wire coming out of the jar will receive a bone-jarring shock if a large enough static charge has been fed into the storage jar. Called a Leyden jar (after the place where it seems most likely to have first been invented), this device was used by Benjamin Franklin in his well-known experiment with the kite. He succeeded in charging up a Leyden jar with a kite flown into an electrical storm. One end of the (wire) kite string is said to have been attached to a key dipped into the water. The experiment demonstrated that the electricity of lightning and the electricity of the laboratory are the same. Why Mr. Franklin was not instantly electrocuted remains a mystery. It definitely is not advisable to attempt to repeat this interesting experiment. The storage battery of Alessandro Volta eventually replaced the Leyden jar, and more adequate devices for generating electrical currents were under development by Faraday and others.

A key element in the inexorable movement of technology toward the electrical telegraph was the development of the electromagnet. By the 1830's, the various technical traits prerequisite to an electrical telegraph were available within the scientific culture. It remained only to put them together in the required pattern. The idea of the sympathetic telegraph had tantalized men for centuries. The need for such a communication device was critical, and the technological base had accumulated to a point where no fundamental problem remained to be solved.

Several people at about the same time seem to have hit upon one scheme or another that would constitute a workable telegraph. But it was the American Samuel F. B. Morse whose patents and system prevailed. Morse, the portrait painter, was not a scientist, and in his *naïveté* he seems to have blundered onto solutions for making a workable telegraph that scientists had overlooked as unlikely possibilities. He had set up a workshop in one of the buildings of the University of the City of New York, where he served as professor of literature and the arts of design. He tinkered with numerous gadgets and frequently sought the advice of several of his somewhat skeptical scientific friends. He eventually worked out a telegraph system that permitted him to transmit messages through ten miles of wire strung around and around in his workshop.

Morse immediately applied for a government grant to enable him to perfect the device (which he had promptly patented). After a great deal of fumbling, hesitation, and delay, the federal government eventually financed a telegraph line between Washington, D.C. and Baltimore, Maryland. The historical message: "What hath God wrought?" flashed between the two cities on May 24, 1844, and the world entered into the era of instantaneous electric communication.

After an initial period of hardship, hesitation, and financial loss, the electric telegraph was gradually accepted by business, the military, and other groups, and the thin wires soon led to most major centers of population. The federal government, which had financed the original long distance line, threw away its opportunity to control the patents and relinquished all its rights. They became the property of private corporations, with Morse as a major stockholder, and the development of this medium was left to private enterprise. It is clear now that the failure of the government to maintain itself in the telegraph business *set a precedent* that would be followed in the United States, where private ownership of the media of public communication constitutes a central condition in determining the type of content which the audiences of the broadcast media now enjoy. It was this seemingly unimportant turn of events that forged an important link in the chain of development of the mass media in this country. As the telephone came, then the wireless telegraph, the wireless telephone, and eventually home broadcasting, the federal government was never again a serious contender for controlling rights to these media (although on one occasion it obtained and relinquished control of radio). This was certainly not the case in other countries.

After conquering tremendous financial and technical problems, cables were laid across the Atlantic Ocean itself by Cyrus W. Field and on July 27, 1866, a message crossed the great sea with incredible speed. Within a very short time, networks of cables were laid under the oceans to the principal population areas of the world. By 1876, Alexander Bell and his brilliant assistant had succeeded in transmitting the human voice over electrical wires, and the pace of cultural accumulation in the area of communication technology was increasing swiftly. Soon the huge cultural lag between communication technology and complexity of social organization would begin to close. From the telegraph and the telephone it was only a short and very natural step to elimination of the wires to achieve a wireless telegraph and eventually a wireless telphone.

ELECTROMAGNETIC RADIATION AND THE WIRELESS TELEGRAPH

While the development of the telegraph had been occurring, scientists like Volta, Ampère, Henry, Faraday, Maxwell, and Hertz were continuously working to understand the basic nature of electricity. The growth of increasingly sophisticated theory permitted an ever more elaborate technology for generating, storing, measuring, transmitting, modifying, and variously harnessing electrical power. Along about the time of the American Civil War, James Maxwell in Scotland had worked out a mathematical theory of mysterious electromagnetic waves which were supposed to travel at the speed of light. By 1888, a young German, Heinrich Hertz, had demonstrated the actual existence of these waves and built a laboratory apparatus for generating them and detecting them. The scientific world became intensely interested in this phenomenon, and experiments with the Hertzian waves were being carried on in laboratories in many countries.

In the early 1890's, Guglielmo Marconi, who was than only twenty years old, became acquainted with these experimental studies of Hertzian waves and the apparatus used to generate and detect them. He reasoned logically that if their distance could be extended beyond the few hundred feet of the laboratory devices, signals in code might be transmitted with them in a kind of telegraph without wires. He promptly purchased an apparatus and began experimenting with it, sending its signals across the garden on his father's estate. Although not a scientist, he was an imaginative tinkerer, and he succeeded in modifying the laboratory device and strengthening it to a point where he could send dot-and-dash messages up to about a mile. His apparatus had become the first wireless telegraph.

Marconi's work was never intended to advance basic science. His experiments had immediate practical and commercial goals rather than theoretical or scientific ones. He hurried to England in 1897 to patent his wireless telegraph. It was essentially a system of fairly common laboratory devices built on a very large scale for sending and receiving the Hertzian waves in the dots and dashes of Morse's telegraph code.

There was a well defined raising of eyebrows among the scientists when they learned that their laboratory gear had found its way into the patent office. Only a few, notably Crookes, Sir Oliver Lodge, and Ernest Rutherford, had given any thought at all to its practical use.[3]

Marconi soon built larger and larger devices that reached out over longer distances. Eventually even the Atlantic was spanned. Although Marconi's work may not have advanced basic science noticeably, it did represent a most significant step in the development of radio as an instantaneous medium of long-range communication. It brought the end product of more than a century of scientific research out of the laboratory and into the hands of groups who desperately needed a device with which to communicate rapidly over long distances.

"Marconi had come to England from Italy because he believed that England with her large mercantile marine, would prove the more profitable market for the discoveries he had made."[4] The wireless was by no means a mass medium at this time. By the end of the first decade of the new century, it was in the hands of commercial, military, and governmental groups for the transmission of confidential information. It was especially suitable for use on ships, which could carry its heavy and bulky apparatus. The general public knew of the wireless telegraph only through what they occasionally read in the newspaper. The thought that they would ever have one in their homes and that it would begin to alter their family's daily routines surely never entered their heads.

FROM WIRELESS TELEGRAPH
TO RADIO TELEPHONE

When radio had proved itself capable of performing the task Marconi and others had envisioned, powerful economic resources were brought to bear upon its development. The British and American Marconi companies soon had strong rivals. The naval establishments of powerful countries lost little time in adopting the wireless. Shipping firms found at last a practical means of keeping in contact with vessels at sea. Inevitably, ships with wireless apparatus found themselves colliding with icebergs or otherwise in difficulties. Dramatic messages of distress brought other ships similarly equipped to the rescue. These events attracted great popular attention. Meanwhile, radio technology continued to develop. Involved legal battles were fought over invention after invention during the time that radio's pioneers were improving the reliability, power, distance, and clarity of wireless messages. International conferences attempted to work out rules governing the transmission and receiving of messages. Hundreds of shore stations were built along coastlines by commercial, marine, and official naval interests. In the years just before World War I, wireless telegraphy was a widely used, commercially sound technique that had substantially begun to close the great cultural lag between communication technology and the development of complex and far-flung social organization. But no one had yet thought of the device as a medium of communication for the ordinary member of society.

The transmission of the human voice by wireless was the next step, and a number of inventors and scientists were working on the idea. It was not really such a tremendously difficult problem. The existing dot-and-dash wireless system had been developed in such a way that it was technically capable of receiving such broadcasts if they could be properly incorporated into the radiated signal. It was on Christmas Eve of 1906 that wireless operators on ships up and down the Atlantic sea lanes off the coast of the United States first heard a human being speak to them through their earphones. They could scarcely believe their ears!

Reginald A. Fessenden had prepared an apparatus that permitted the broadcasting of infinitely more complex signals than those of the simple tone of the dot and dash. He had also constructed a very powerful transmitter to use in his experiments. Several persons spoke over the wireless on that eventful evening; one made a speech, one read a poem, and one even played the violin. The radio telephone had become a reality.

In spite of Fessenden's early success with radio telephony, it was to be many years before Americans had regularly scheduled radio programs to listen to in their own homes. Yet, there was a growing popular interest in radio. In that same year, 1906, it was discovered that several mineral substances were capable of detecting radio transmissions when used in an extremely simple circuit. A very inexpensive "crystal set" radio receiver could be built by almost anyone with elementary mechanical skills. The cost of the parts was insignificant. This meant that people all over the country, even youngsters, could listen in on the code signals in the air. Once the code was learned, the sport had great appeal, and one never knew when he might eavesdrop upon an agonized signal of distress from some vessel sinking in mid-ocean.

Thus at the very period when it was important that the general public be educated to the possibilities of radio the efficient crystal detector came along to boost the industry. The Morse code had great appeal to boys and young men, but when music and spoken words might occasionally be picked up out of the ether there arose a veritable army of enthusiasts for the new science. Boys love to tinker, to experiment with chemistry or mechanics, and here was the opportunity of the ages.[5]

The first decade of the new century brought many refinements, improvements, and significant new ideas. One of these was to revolutionize radio broadcasting and was even to provide the basis of an entire electronics industry that would follow. Its inventor, Lee De Forest, called it an *audion;* in the technical jargon of early radio it was called a *valve;* today we would call it a *vacuum tube.* Only recently has it been displaced by the transistor, a device which performs approximately the same task. De Forest's audion was the key element in electronic amplifiers that could enlarge both broadcast and received radio signals. After refinement, it permitted the human voice to be transmitted to all parts of the globe. Radio receivers became far more reliable and the clarity of reception improved. Refinement followed refinement. The heterodyne circuit and superheterodyne circuit significantly improved reception. Radio equipment, which was once so huge and heavy that only ships could easily transport it, now became increasingly light and portable. In fact during World War I, radio telephones were successfully mounted in airplanes for the purpose of informing gun batteries on the ground of the accuracy of their fire.

In some ways, one of the most crippling of the social conditions surrounding the early development of radio was the concept of private ownership and the profit motive. Every minor and major invention was immediately patented in the United States, in Britain, and in other countries as well. It became nearly impossible to make needed improvements in radio components or to market equipment thus improved without falling into bitter court entanglements over patent claims. In fact, all of the major pioneers in radio, from Marconi on, frequently found themselves battling each other in court. Lee De Forest, one of the principal inventors of major radio components, was actually arrested and charged with fraud. The problem was, of course, that there were fortunes to be made in wireless, and the competition to tie up important inventions for exploitation was intense.

At the same time, it is also true that millions of dollars were expended by private individuals and syndicates to aid inventors in improving their ideas to the point where they could be turned into marketable devices. In the final analysis, this financial support for research may have compensated for the many problems that the concepts of private ownership, corporate profit, and commercial exploitation brought to radio.

World War I brought urgent military needs for the improvement of radio systems. It brought not only new organization, manpower, and funds to bear upon unsolved technical problems, but it had another important effect. All patent litigation and restrictions were temporarily suspended for the duration of the war. The federal government was in complete control of the infant industry, and this brought new cooperative efforts to the task of technical advancement which would have taken much longer in peacetime.

The Radio Music Box

A young radio engineer by the name of David Sarnoff had been rapidly advanced in the ranks of the American Marconi Company. He had achieved considerable public attention during the sinking of the ill-famed *Titanic* when she was ripped by an iceberg in mid-Atlantic. David Sarnoff remained at his telegraph key in a radio station in New York City decoding messages from the disaster scene. For three days and three nights he kept a horrified public apace of developments concerning the tragic incident. He was later moved up from this post to more important positions in the company. In 1916, Mr. Sarnoff sent a memorandum to his superiors. This now-famous memorandum in a sense did for radio what Benjamin Day did for the press almost a century earlier. It showed an economically profitable way by which radio could be used as a medium of mass communication for ordinary families. While the company did not immediately follow Mr. Sarnoff's advice, he successfully predicted the major outlines of radio as a mass medium (he wrote):

I have in mind a plan of development which would make radio a "household utility" in the same sense as the piano or phonograph. The idea is to bring music into the house by wireless.

While this has been tried in the past by wires, it has been a failure because wires do not lend themselves to this scheme. With radio, however, it would be entirely feasible. For example—a radio telephone transmitter having a range of say 25 to 50 miles can be installed at a fixed point where instrumental or vocal music or both are produced. ... The receiver can be designed in the form of a simple "Radio Music Box" and arranged for several different wave lengths, which should be changeable with the throwing of a single switch or pressing of a single button.

The "Radio Music Box" can be supplied with amplifying tubes and a loudspeaking telephone, all of which can be neatly mounted in one box. The box can be placed on a table in the parlor or living room, the switch set accordingly and the transmitted music received. . . .

The same principle can be extended to numerous other fields as, for example, receiving lectures at home which can be made perfectly audible; also events of national importance can be simultaneously announced and received. Baseball scores can be transmitted in the air by the use of one set installed at the Polo Grounds. The same would be true of other cities. This proposition would be especially interesting to farmers and others living in outlying districts removed from the cities. By the purchase of a "Radio Music Box" they could enjoy concerts, lectures, music, recitals, etc. While I have indicated a few of the most probable fields of usefulness for such a device yet there are numerous other fields to which the principle can be extended.[6]

If Mr. Sarnoff had added the singing commercial and the soap opera, his description of radio as it would develop into a system of mass communication would have been almost perfect. Within ten years he was to see radio grow into a medium for household use, following almost to the letter the outline that he had dictated. David Sarnoff's suggested application of existing radio technology to this imaginative, new, and practical usage ranks as an insight with that of Marconi's idea of taking existing laboratory devices and using them as a wireless telegraph. Sarnoff himself played a major role in bringing about this transformation; he became in a short time the manager of a new corporation in the radio field and was able to help make his dream become a reality.

Feeble attempts to perpetuate governmental control over radio at the close of the Great War were crushed by outcries by private interests. Just as the federal government had allowed control of the telegraph to fall into the hands of private persons, it similarly handed over this important new medium of public communication to commercial interests. Radio was defined by this act as an *arena of business competition* as opposed to a public medium of communication to be operated by organizations of government. This decision was to have far-reaching effects and ramifications with which we live today. Other societies formulated different definitions concerning the control of broadcasting, and the systems of broadcasting that have developed in such countries as Great Britain, the Soviet Union, and others offer interesting contrasts with our own. That is not to say that they are better, only that they are very different due largely to historical reasons.

Once direct governmental control was eliminated, British and American commercial interests, which had prospered during the war, fought each other to gain control. The General Electric Company finally bought up the British shares of American Marconi and formed a new corporation with a patriotic name (apparently designed to dispel fears of foreign control). The new Radio Corporation of America (RCA) was able to consolidate a number of conflicting patent interests, and it gave control over wireless telegraphy and radio broadcasting in the United States to American stockholders. In 1919, David Sarnoff, who had forecast the "Radio Music Box," was appointed its first commercial manager.

COMMERCIAL BROADCASTING BEGINS

Shortly after World War I, the Westinghouse Company, a major American manufacturer of electrical equipment, attempted to move into the international wireless telegraph field. It was not particularly successful. This was due largely to the fact that its rival RCA owned most of the important patents. However, some of its directors were interested in the newer field of wireless telephony, and the company had done considerable research in this area. Dr. Frank Conrad was in charge of experiments with new and powerful transmitters of this type. In connection with this work, he not only built such a transmitter for experiments at the Westinghouse laboratory, but he constructed one at home over his garage so that he could continue his work in the evening. He licensed his home transmitter nearly a year later as station 8XK in April, 1920. He started to broadcast signals during the evening hours as he worked with his apparatus in attempts to improve its design. He soon found that people in the area were listening in on their amateur receiving sets. This proved to be a boon at first, because their letters, cards, and phone calls gave him some indication of the range and clarity of his transmitter. Before long, however, his circle of amateur radio listeners began to become a problem. To create a continuous sound, he had started to play the victrola over the air. His listeners began to demand particular songs and would even call him at odd hours to ask him to play a favorite record. Dr. Conrad solved the problem by regularizing his broadcasts, and with the cooperation of a local phonograph dealer, he was able to present continuous music for a two-hour period two evenings a week. The number of listeners grew rapidly, and his family enthusiastically joined in the fun to become the first "disc jockies."

All of this activity increased the demand for receiving sets in the area, and it became increasingly clear that there might be money to be made in the manufacture of such sets for home use. The commercial possibilities of this did not escape the attention of officials of the Westinghouse Company. They decided to build a larger transmitter in East Pittsburgh for the purpose of stimulating the sale of home receivers of their own make and the sale of the components from which amateurs built such sets. It was in this way that Station KDKA, Pittsburgh, came into existence in the year 1920.

Although David Sarnoff had forecast the radio music box several years earlier, it was the decision of Harry P. Davis, vice-president of the Westinghouse Electric and Manufacturing Company, which concretely gave birth to commercial household radio. He decided that a regular transmitting station, operated by the manufacturer of receivers, would create enough interest in the sale of sets to justify the expense of operating the station. Although this financial basis for broadcasting has long since been replaced by the sale of air time for advertising, it was sufficiently practical at the time to get radio started as a mass medium.

To stimulate interest in the new station and, of course, to promote the sale of receiving sets, it was announced that the transmitter would broadcast the results of the 1920 Presidential election over the air. Bulletins were phoned to the station from a nearby newspaper, and the returns were broadcast during the evening of November 11 as they came in. An audience of between five hundred and a thousand people heard the word through the air that Warren G. Harding had been elected President of the United States. The event was a sensation; the dream of David Sarnoff had become a reality.

The Pittsburgh experiment was so successful that other stations were quickly launched. Transmitters began regular broadcasts in New York in 1921, followed by stations in Newark and other cities. Westinghouse soon had several competitors. The public's interest in radio had been growing. Its appetites for the new signals in the air had been whetted by the glamor and excitement of radio's brief history. The dramatic stories of rescues at sea, of daring flights over no-man's-land with radio telephones, and the struggles of giant corporations to gain control over wireless telegraphy had all contributed to this surging interest. When radio stations actually began to broadcast during regular periods with music and voices they could receive at home in their own cities, this latent interest suddenly burst into a full blown craze. The public begin to clamor for radio. By 1922, the manufacture of home receivers was lagging hopelessly behind the receipt of orders. New stations were being built at a staggering pace. In the last half of 1921 licenses were issued for thirty-two new stations, but in the first half of 1922, this number had risen to 254! Although there were still many problems to work out concerning its financial base, its content, and its technical functioning, radio as a mass medium was off to a flying start.

THE EARLY DAYS OF RADIO AS A MASS MEDIUM; THE PROBLEMS OF INTERFERENCE AND FINANCE

One of the earliest problems which household radio encountered was brought on because of its own popularity. There is a limited spectrum of frequencies available that are suitable for broadcasting. In the beginning, no attempts were made by either government or private groups to regulate the frequencies transmitters in a given area would use. The Radio Act of 1912 did not specify frequencies for privately operated broadcast stations. The Secretary of Commerce, who licensed all new transmitters, had selected two frequencies, 750 kilocycles and 833 kilocycles. All stations were assigned one or the other. As the number of transmitters operating grew quickly, there developed an annoying number of instances where two stations were operating near enough to each other so that the program of one would be imposed upon the sound of the other. This type of interference could not easily be controlled. Many stations worked out gentlemen's agreements to divide up available time. There was no legal authority that could assign different positions on the radio band for every station to use and could rigorously enforce such regulations. Obviously, such a problem could be handled only by some form of governmental agency, but there was no adequate provision by Congress or by the states for such a controlling body. The Department of Commerce issued licenses to operate transmitters, but did little else. Because of the lack of control over this technical problem, confusion began to mount.

In the meantime, radio was advancing at a tremendous pace. In 1922, station WJZ in Newark successfully broadcast the World Series. Stations began to broadcast opera, concerts, news, dance music, lectures, church services, and a great variety of events. Voluntary experiments were tried by having nearby stations broadcast on wave lengths at least twenty meters different from each other as a means of avoiding overlap. In spite of efforts to combat interference, the problem continued to grow.

Successful experimentation with networks was tried, and it was found that several stations linked by wires could simultaneously broadcast the same program. The rush to build new transmitters continued, and by 1923 stations were to be found in most major cities across the nation.

But two major problems continued to plague the medium. The technical problem of interference was already badly out of hand, but there was also the problem of paying for the broadcasts. While the larger electrical manufacturers could afford to finance their stations out of their profits on the sale of sets, this was a limited expedient at best, and it was no help at all to the owners of stations who were not electrical manufacturers.

By the end of 1923, some of the initial enthusiasm for constructing radio transmitters began to sag as the hard financial facts had to be faced. There was simply no profit in broadcasting as such, and only those with other financial resources were in positions to continue in operation.

Now that a full year of nation-wide radio broadcasting had been completed the summer of 1923 afforded an opportunity to cast up the accounts, so to speak. This was indeed a disturbing experience, since the studio ledgers of every station disclosed entries almost entirely in the red ink. Fortunes had been squandered in the mad rush. . . . As early as December, 1922, the Department of Commerce reported the suspension of twenty stations for that month alone. With every succeeding month the casualty list had grown more appalling. Between March 19 and April 30, 1923, forty-two stations gave up their franchises. In the month of May there were 26 failures. June, 1923, saw fifty radio stations become silent. In July twenty-five franchises were surrendered. Thus in the period from March 19th to July 31st of this fateful year 143 radio stations went out of business.[7]

Unless some viable financial basis could be found, radio as a medium of communication to the American home was doomed.

But the public was not to be denied radio. The mid-1920's were years of prosperity for most Americans. The grim remembrances of the Great War were fading, and the nation was entering a period of industrial and financial growth. The new practice of installment buying was part of a great expansion of credit which was taking place in the entire economic structure. No one had any inkling of the eventual collapse that would begin in October of 1929. Installment buying made it easier for families of modest means to purchase consumer goods such as radio receivers. Radio listening was becoming increasingly popular, and pressure was being exerted on the Secretary of Commerce, Herbert Hoover, to do something about the interference problem. He did work out a system for assigning different wave lengths to various broadcasting stations, but the attempt to implement it was not completely successful. People who owned sets capable of picking up only one major frequency did not like the idea. Also, there was no actual way of enforcing the assignments, and some transmitters simply ignored the plan. On the other hand, many of the major stations, which were engaged in regular broadcasting, tried to follow the Secretary's assignments and did so with success.

The industry itself was exerting great pressure upon the Department of Commerce not only to regulate frequencies, but to limit the number of stations that could be licensed in a given area. The public, too, was becoming disenchanted with the cacophony that came out of their sets night after night. The problem of interference was getting un-bearable. Ancient spark transmitters used for marine broadcasts, Morse code amateurs, powerful stations which broadcast regularly, and local fly-by-night operators were all blasting each other over the air waves.

Four major conferences were held yearly (1922–1925) in Washington, D.C. to discuss the problems of broadcasting. The position of govern-ment was that it was up to the industry itself to clean up its own house. The newspapers had gotten along without government control. In fact they had fought it bitterly. The film industry was cleaning up its products. In a political system which stressed private initiative, it was felt by many government officials that federal control over broad-casting would be a dangerous precedent. In fact, Congress had repeat-edly refused to consider bills on the subject. The only legislation in existence on radio was the old Radio Act of 1912, which was hope-lessly out of date.

The problem was not an easy one to solve, even by government control. Since wireless telegraphy would also need regulation, the matter had international complications. In addition, there were the thousands of amateurs whose rights had to be protected. Not only were there more than 500 major stations operating on a regular basis, but there were approximately 1,400 small stations of very low wattage that operated when their owners had the urge. Yet, to pick up this jumble of signals, Americans spent 136 million dollars for receiving sets in 1923 alone.[8]

The Secretary of Commerce struggled valiantly to find a solution. He tried limiting the power and hours of operation of some stations so that they could share a given frequency. By 1925, every spot on the frequency band was occupied, some by several stations. The broadcast band could not conveniently be extended without severely infringing upon other important kinds of radio and wireless operations. There were 175 additional stations clamoring for licenses that could not be accommodated.

In 1926, this arbitrary control system collapsed. A federal court decided that the Secretary of Commerce had no legal basis to impose any restrictions on a station's power, hours of operation, or trans-mitting frequency. In that same year also, the Attorney General issued the opinion that the only existing legislation, the Radio Act of 1912, really did not provide a legal basis for any of the regulations he had been using. Mr. Hoover simply had to abandon the entire attempt in disgust, and he issued a public statement that urged radio stations to regulate themselves. They were unable to do so.

In the face of the utter chaos that followed, President Coolidge asked Congress to enact appropriate legislation to regulate broadcasting, including provisions for adequate enforcement. They did so in 1927. They first enunciated the important principle that *the air waves belong to the people,* and that they can be used by private individuals only with the formal permission of government on a short-term license basis. Licenses were to be granted or revoked when it was in the public interest, convenience, or necessity to do so. All licenses of existing stations were automatically revoked; and the industry had to start all over by applying formally for a franchise to operate and by providing adequate statements and explanations as to why it would be in the public interest for them to do so.

The Radio Act of 1927 was to be a temporary solution. After a seven-year period of observation, trial, and some readjustments, a new and more permanent set of statutes was written and a Federal Communciations Commission (FCC) was established to enforce the provisions. The Federal Communications Act of 1934 has since become, with appropriate amendment from time to time, the principal regulating instrument for the broadcasting industry in the United States.

Meanwhile, the boisterous new industry continued to seek an adequate means of financial support. By the mid-1920's, broadcasters were still grappling with this problem. A committee of New York business men tried the experiment of soliciting funds directly from the listening audience for the purpose of hiring high quality talent to perform over one of the larger stations in the area. While a trickle of funds came in, most listeners decided they would rather listen free to whatever happened to come their way than pay directly out of pocket to be assured of higher quality programs. This response typifies the feelings of the majority even today. It also explains in part why the public eventually accepted advertising messages as a means of financing broadcasting. They would rather put up with somewhat objectionable commercials than pay directly for their entertainment.

Other schemes were proposed. David Sarnoff felt that wealthy philanthropists should endow radio stations just as they did universities, hospitals, or libraries. Others suggested charging a license fee for operating a home receiver, the proceeds of which were to be divided among broadcasters. Many felt that the industry itself would solve the problem. The larger manufacturers of receiving sets were said to have an obligation to provide something to hear on their products. It was thought that this would eventually result in a small number of networks, each operated by a different manufacturer or group of manufacturers and that there would be few if any independent stations.

But while these debates were being carried on, advertising was quietly creeping in as a dependable source of revenue for radio broadcasts. In fact, as early as 1922, station WEAF had sold radio time for ten minute talks on behalf of a Long Island real estate company which was selling lots. Then major companies began to sponsor programs. A department store paid for an hour-long musical program. A tobacco company sponsored a radio variety show. A candy company presented two comedians. The public was much drawn to these, and audiences wanted more. At first, these sponsors made no direct advertising appeal for their products. They simply mentioned their name as sponsor or titled the program after the name of their product. This form of subtle advertising found little criticism. The general goal of sponsoring such a program was to create good will among the audience.

The Secretary of Commerce was dead set against open huckstering on radio. He said, "it is inconceivable that we should allow so great a possibility for service, for news, for entertainment, and for vital commercial purposes to be drowned in advertising chatter." [9] Many other voices were added to this view. Responsible officials in government, leaders of the industry, and many groups of listeners concurred.

But in our society, such an idealistic position was doomed from the outset. With listeners more interested in "free" entertainment than quality programming; with government playing only a technical role, primarily to keep frequencies unscrambled; with ownership of the media in the hands of profit-seeking companies and corporations, the noble views of the Secretary of Commerce and his supporters were not consistent with the value system, the political structure, and the economic institution of the society within which the new medium was developing. The same socioeconomic forces that led newspapers to turn to selling space to advertisers so they could sell their products to a mass audience were to result in a parallel pattern for radio. The surrender to advertising was strongly resisted for some time, but inevitably it came. It was somewhat artificially held back briefly by the policies of the American Telephone and Telegraph Company, which controlled many patents, transmission lines, and radio equipment used by broadcasters. But even this opposition was relaxed, and the way was opened for the flood of commercial messages that are now so much a part of broadcasting in the United States.

At first, advertising was restrained and dignified. But soon it became increasingly direct and to the point. It would be incorrect to say the public welcomed advertising, but it is certainly true it welcomed what advertising revenues made possible. The public was willing to hear the sponsor's pitch in order to be able to listen to his program. One reason for this was that programs were quickly designed to have great popular appeal. Money from advertising made it possible to hire effective talent. Individual comedians, singers, and bands soon developed large and enthusiastic followings. Weekly drama programs became popular. Programs for children were developed; sports broadcasts drew large audiences. A great variety of content was designed to capture the interest of different large components of the population.

By the end of the decade, the major problems of radio as a mass medium of communication were solved. The homeowner could buy a reasonably priced and reliable receiving set on time payments. The broadcaster received generous profits from selling his time to advertisers; sponsors sold products effectively over the air to a mass market; and talent with great popular appeal captured the nightly attention of the public. In the background, the new federal legislation had brought order out of chaos with respect to the interference problem. Only the ominous event of the crash of 1929 threatened to muddy the picture. But as it turned out, this was to have little negative impact upon the growth of radio.

The Golden Age of Radio

Radio flowered during the 1930's and the 1940's. These were very trying decades for the American society. The great depression and World War II were events that affected the destinies of every citizen, but they had little inhibiting effect on radio.

An overview of radio's growth in the American society can be obtained from Table 4, which shows the number of receiving sets in operation for selected years. By the end of the 1930's there was slightly more than one set per household in the United States. This remarkable growth in the use of radio receivers had occurred in spite of ten years of economic depression following the stock market collapse of '29. It should be emphasized for those who did not experience those tragic days that this was a period of great distress for American families. The pathos of an era when heads of families were unable to find employment and when there were few public agencies to turn to for

TABLE 4

THE GROWTH OF RADIO SET OWNERSHIP IN THE UNITED STATES
(1922–1967)

Year	Total Number of Sets	Total Number of Households	Sets Per Household
1922	400,000	25,687,000	.016
1925	4,000,000	27,540,000	.145
1930	13,000,000	29,997,000	.433
1935	30,500,000	31,892,000	.956
1940	51,000,000	35,153,000	1.451
1945	56,000,000	37,503,000	1.493
1950	98,000,000	43,554,000	2.250
1955	135,000,000	47,788,000	2.825
1960	156,000,000	52,799,000	2.955
1965	227,000,000	57,251,000	3.965
1967	268,000,000	58,845,000	4.554

SOURCES: New York World Telegram Corporation, *The World Almanac,
1969* (New York, 1969), p. 62.

U.S. Bureau of Census, *Historical Statistics of the United States, Colonial
Times to 1957* (Washington, D.C., 1960), Series A 242–244, p. 15.

U.S. Bureau of Census, *Current Population Reports: Population Characteristics,* Series P 20, No. 106 (January 9, 1961), p. 11; No. 119 (September 19, 1962), p. 4; No. 166 (August 4, 1967), p. 4.

NOTE: Figures after 1960 include Alaska and Hawaii. Figures for 1960 have
been revised from the first edition because of revisions in source materials.

relief cannot be adequately appreciated without having been personally involved. It was a time when the people of the United States were
gravely depressed in spirit as well as in an economic sense.

But in spite of the hardships of the times, radio seemed to thrive on
the depression! Advertising revenues, instead of drying up, grew at
an ever increasing pace. The number of radio sets owned by Americans about doubled every five years. Families who had reached the
limit of their financial resources would scrape together enough money
to have their radio receiver repaired if it broke down. They might
have to let the furniture go back to the finance company or to stall
the landlord for the rent, but they hung grimly on to their radio sets.

Radio fit the needs of millions of hard-pressed people during that
trying time. It had music to restore their sagging spirits, funny men to
cheer them up, and dramatic news to divert their attention from their
personal problems. Amateur nights, evening dramas, soap operas,
Western adventures, and variety shows were all followed avidly by
loyal listeners night after night. On a summer night a person could
walk down a street on the evening that a particularly popular come-

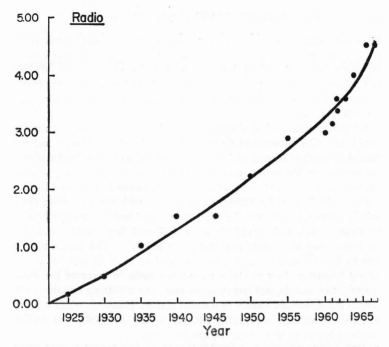

FIGURE 3. The Cumulative Diffusion Curve for Radio; Ownership of
Receiving Sets Per Household in the United States (1922–1965)

dian was on the air and hear the program uninterrupted through the
open windows of every house he passed.

By the time the depression eased and the war was about to begin,
radio was reaching every ear. In mid-1940, there were nearly one and
a half sets per household in the United States. Radio had also become
increasingly sophisticated in every sense. It was technically excellent.
It was possible for direct broadcasts to be picked up and relayed to
listeners in their homes from almost any point on the globe. News
broadcasting had become a sophisticated art, and outstanding journalists had established themselves within this new medium. The press
and radio had learned to live with each other after prolonged feuding,
and radio had full access to the world's wire services.

During World War II, the radio industry made all of its resources
available to the federal government. War information messages, domestic propaganda, the selling of war bonds, campaigns to reduce the
civilian usage of important materials, and many other vital services
were performed. It should be noted that the manufacture of home
receiving sets was completely curtailed during the war years. Figure 3,

the cumulative diffusion curve for radio sets, shows that from 1940 to 1945 no new sets were acquired by American households. Special attention should be called, however, to the sharp rise in sales during the following five-year period, when the cumulative diffusion curve recovered from the retardation of the war years and resumed its regular pattern of growth.

Of greater sociological significance are the postwar years when radio was faced with vigorous competition from television. If radio had retained its original format and content, it would have remained a direct competitor of the newer medium, which was apparently capable of gratifying the relevant needs of the mass audience in a more effective manner. At first, radio attempted to do this with the somewhat optimistic argument that over the years people had built up a deep loyalty to radio, which had served them so well, and they could not easily be lured away to a flashy new thing like television. The public turned out to be completely fickle, however, and as soon as families could afford television, they gleefully abandoned radio in favor of the tube. To put it in sociological terms, radio had been satisfying certain needs within the American society as a social system. However, when a more effective functional alternative became widely available, the earlier medium began to show signs of obsolescence.

Faced with the prospect of oblivion, radio was forced to find audience needs to satisfy that were not being effectively served by television. It successfully found such needs, and radio remodeled itself along new lines. During the 30's, 40's, and even the early 50's, radio had successfully captured the attentions of the American family during the major evening hours, and they turned to their radio to listen to the country's most popular entertainers. As television grew, it took over these entertainers along with the family's evening time. Radio was displaced from the living room and had to be content with the bedroom, the kitchen, the automobile, and the beach. Transistor technology, which opened up a huge market for miniature sets, helped keep radio from the type of postwar decline that occurred with motion picture theaters as a result of television (Figure 2).

At present, radio seems to have found a workable formula. It caters to its audience during times when television is inappropriate. People listen when they wake up in the morning, while they are working, driving, playing, etc. But when evening comes and they settle down in their living rooms, the radio dial is turned off and the television set is warmed up. Radio remains as one of the most massive of our mass media in terms of the ownership of sets. Table 4 shows that

Americans now own more than four sets per household. Figure 3 suggests that the curve of diffusion for radio has not yet begun to level off; it has by no means reached its peak. The trend toward miniaturization will probably continue and set ownership will soar even higher. Needless to say, the impressive number of sets owned by American families does not imply that they spend a corresponding amount of time in radio listening.

THE DEVELOPMENT OF TELEVISION

The newest of the broadcast media inherited many of the traditions of radio. Several factors worked together to make its technological development and its diffusion through the American society a much more rapid and less chaotic process than was the case with its parent medium. The technology of television was really quite sophisticated before mass manufactured sets were placed on the market for the public. There was no period comparable to the "crystal set" era in any widespread sense. The new medium did not have to work out a structure of control with the government. The FCC and its supporting legislation were simply taken over from radio. The financial basis of television was clear from the start. The public was completely accustomed to "commercials," and television promised to be even more effective as a vehicle for the sales pitch. No great problem was foreseen in attracting advertising money. There was no period of feuding with newspaper and wire service interests. These arrangements were simply extended from established radio interests. The network idea was already popular from the older medium. An adequate coaxial cable technology was available and only the physical facilities needed to be constructed. The public was already completely familiar with the moving picture, and its transmission through broadcasting was not difficult for them to accept. For this reason, little public resistance to adoption of the new device was anticipated.

Actually, the television set quickly became a status symbol. In its early period of diffusion, families who could ill afford a set would sometimes scrimp on necessities to be able to buy one. The "easy payment plan," by now a deeply established American folkway, was widely used by families of modest means to acquire their sets. The urge to be identified as a set owner in the initial period of diffusion was so strong that in some cases families are said to have purchased and installed television antennae conspicuously on top of their dwellings long before they actually had sets to hook on. Stories of this type were widely circulated during the late 1940's. The definition of the television set as a luxury and as a status symbol led to occasional public outrage when it was discovered that people on public welfare or other forms of relief owned sets. Apparently the experiences of the depression years when radio sets were regarded as extremely comforting to people in trying economic circumstances had been forgotten.

Actually, television might have been a household medium even earlier had it not been for World War II. The electronic technology of television was worked out during the 1920's and the 30's. By 1939, television broadcasts were being made in the United States. The World's Fair of that year featured demonstrations of this latest marvel of science, and President Roosevelt gave an address over the new communication medium. This particular broadcast was viewed by only a handful, because commercial manufacturers had not yet begun to mass-produce sets. In 1941, on the eve of World War II, the FCC approved home television, and the communication industry began to work out elaborate plans for its development. By this time there were nearly 5,000 television sets (mostly in the New York area) in private hands, and several small stations were broadcasting regularly for two or three hours a day.

World War II interrupted any further development for the duration. In some ways this block to development may have accounted for the very rapid growth of television when the country returned to a peace-time economy. Electronics manufacturing techniques that aided in overcoming problems of television receiver production were developed during the war. Furthermore, the war completely ended the depression of the prewar period. In fact, with minor fluctuations the country entered a period of continuous economic growth, which has been almost uninterrupted for more than two decades. The purchasing power of the average family rose to a point where television ownership was within the means of almost everyone.

THE FREEZE

With the bitter lessons of the interference chaos in the early days of radio before them, the government took a much more active role in controlling the broadcasting frequencies of television. By 1948 there were about seventy stations in operation and several million sets in use. Applications for new permits began to come in rapidly. Since television has only thirteen VHF channels for the whole nation, a rigorous means of control was needed to avoid interference. Fortunately, the television signal does not follow the curvature of the earth as does a radio signal. This meant that two stations broadcasting on the same channel would not interfere with each other if there were sufficient distance between them. A master plan for the whole United States had to be worked out so television channels could be fairly allocated. There was also the need to study competing color systems to see what problems lay there. In addition, there were a substantial number of UHF channels on the spectrum, and these had to be allocated among competing interests. With these and other technical problems in mind, the FCC stopped granting new permits for television stations in 1948. Those stations in operation were permitted to continue, but time was needed to work out a master plan in detail so that as many problems as possible would be avoided when television reached its maturity. Actually, the stations already in operation (about seventy) were located in urban centers and were concentrated in the more eastern, and therefore more populated, sections of the country. Thus, the sale of sets could continue, even though no new stations were being built. In spite of this "freeze," which continued until 1952, the sale of sets rose steadily. Table 5 shows that the number of sets owned in the United States was only two for every hundred households in 1948, but in 1951, before the freeze was lifted, this had increased to about thirty-five per hundred. When the freeze was discontinued, a large number of applications for stations were received, and areas of the United States that had been without a television signal began to find television stations in their midst. These factors stimulated the sale of sets, and Figure 4 shows that the period 1952 to 1954 was one of very rapid diffusion. By the mid-1960's television had virtually reached saturation in the American society. There are still pockets where television has not penetrated, both in terms of the social structure and with respect to geographical location. Among extremely low income areas of the Appalachians, for example, television ownership is the exception rather than the rule. This is due in some part to the difficulties of capturing the signal in a mountainous area, but it is also due to simple lack of money. A recent study of relief recipients among former coal miners in eastern Kentucky showed the median annual income of such families is approximately 700 dollars.[10] These depressed groups have counterparts in urban areas and in many other rural regions of the country. Such families have very limited contact with the mass culture of the television complex. In another study of rural farm families in this same region, it was discovered in 1965 that about one head-of-household in five did not really comprehend the most elemen-

TABLE 5

THE GROWTH OF TELEVISION SET OWNERSHIP IN THE UNITED STATES
(1946–1967)

Year	Monochrome Sets in Use (in Thousands)	Color Sets in Use (in Thousands)	Total Number of Households (in Thousands)	Monochrome Sets Per Household	Color Sets Per Household
1946	8		38,370	.0002	
1947	250		39,107	.0064	
1948	1,000		40,523	.0247	
1949	4,000		42,182	.0948	
1950	10,500		43,554	.2411	
1951	15,750		44,656	.3527	
1953	28,000		46,334	.6043	
1957	47,200		49,543	.9527	
1960	55,500	200	52,799	1.0512	.0038
1961	57,600	400	53,464	1.0774	.0075
1962	60,800	800	54,652	1.1125	.0146
1963	65,000	1,600	55,189	1.1778	.0290
1964	70,000	3,000	55,996	1.2501	.0536
1965	75,000	5,000	57,251	1.3100	.0873
1966	78,500	9,700	58,092	1.3513	.1670
1967	81,500	12,700	58,845	1.3850	.2158

SOURCES: U.S. Bureau of Census, *Historical Statistics of the United States,
Colonial Times to 1957* (Washington, D.C., 1960), Series A 242–244, p. 15.

U.S. Bureau of Census, *Current Population Reports, Population Characteristics,* Series P 20, No. 106 (January 9, 1961), p. 11; No. 119 (September 19, 1962), p. 4; No. 166 (August 4, 1967), p. 4.

New York World-Telegram Corporation, *The World Almanac, 1969*
(New York, 1969), p. 62.

NOTE: All figures after 1960 include Alaska and Hawaii.

tary ideas of atomic warfare. For example, they could not explain
even in the most simple way the idea of "atomic fallout." [11] Such
families simply are not part of the tidal wave of mass communication
that engulfs the nation daily. They are isolated not only from television
but from other forms of mass communication as well.

At the other extreme is a hardy band who resist television on the
grounds that it is culturally degrading and absorbs time that could
be put to more constructive use. Some families try to shield their
children from "infection" by the tube. There are indications that the
resistance of such groups is weakening as television viewing becomes
more and more of a standard folkway in the society.

The final outlines of television in the United States are by no means

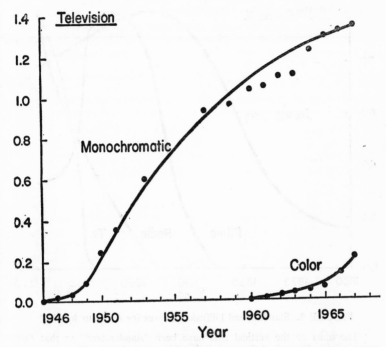

FIGURE 4.   The Cumulative Diffusion Curve for Television; Ownership of Receiving Sets Per Household in the United States (1946–1967)

perfectly clear. In the opinion of many manufacturers, color sets well begin more rapid diffusion as the price comes down. Technical advances have improved color reception, and current technology is not likely to change drastically for some years. These factors should increase adoption. Another perplexing problem is the place of subscription television. There is clearly a portion of the population who are dissatisfied with current popular fare on television and who are also sufficiently affluent to pay for better programs. "Pay" television has not been a popular idea with the general public, however, many of whom seem to see it as some kind of threat to the "free" television which they now enjoy. Similarly, educational television is a confusing issue. Many residents of a community without an educational television channel bitterly complain about it. However, when such a channel begins to operate in their city, many of those who formerly complained do not view it.

One of the most constant factors about our electronic mass media

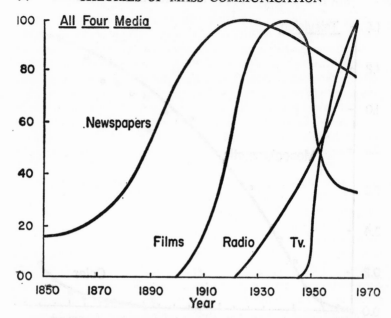

FIGURE 5. Standardized Diffusion Curves for All Four Media *

* The units on the vertical axis have been "standardized" so that each curve reaches its peak at the same point. This procedure facilitates comparison of one curve with another.

is their continuous change. The television set of today is a vastly different object from what people were viewing in the late 1940's. The sets that will be used in the late 1970's and 80's will make present equipment appear quaint and amusing. Television may not be the final of the mass media. Devices for printing newspapers or even magazines in the home are under study. Special tapes to play over a home television set are already available, although at great cost. As electronic technology continues to advance, media that are beyond our imagination may become as commonplace in the future as a radio receiver or a television set is today.

As each of our mass media was invented and converted to a form suitable for use by American families, it was diffused more or less rapidly throughout the population. Figure 5 shows the diffusion curves of the four media discussed in the present text. For each curve, units on the vertical axis have been standardized by means of a simple percentage conversion. This facilitates direct comparisons between curves. The longer adoption period of the newspaper stands in contrast to the swift diffusion of television. The decline of the newspaper reveals the impact of functional alternatives. The drastic reduction in motion picture attendance indicates what happens when a new medium becomes capable of gratifying the entertainment needs of a society in a more effective way. Clearly, the older media are showing signs of obsolescence, while the newer electronic media have not yet reached their maximum points of diffusion. However, as even newer media are invented, different patterns of usage can be expected to emerge.

The foregoing chapters on the newspaper, the film, radio, and television have attempted to show some of the details concerning the impact of a society on its mass media. The study of the media within this perspective emphasizes their background in terms of the accumulation of technological culture traits. It notes their invention as new configurations of such traits. It follows their transformation from technical devices known only to a few to forms which can be used by the multitude. It traces their diffusion patterns as they spread through the society and studies their curves of obsolescence as they are replaced by functional alternatives. This type of analysis says little about the psychological processes of individuals as they decided to adopt the various media or as they were influenced by the absorption of media content. Such an analysis does stress the broad social, economic, political, demographic, and other changes that characterize the society during the development of each medium. Such factors as war, depression, affluence, immigration, urbanization, the spread of education, and the presence of given technological elements in the culture of a society can facilitate, inhibit, or otherwise affect the development and adoption of a given mass medium.

The spread of the media is a set of social events which offer important data to the student of social change as well as to those whose interest is more specifically in communication. No medium of mass communication exists in a social vacuum. It is linked inextricably to complex and changing cultural constraints. The older idea that the media are independent forces, shaping and molding the society as they wish, is simplistic and outmoded. The development of a given medium and what it presents to society are dependent not only upon the characteristics of the medium itself, but upon the salient norms and values of the socio-cultural system within which it operates. In other words, there are numerous and pervasive ways in which a society has a profound influence upon its media.

Chapter V

ELEMENTARY CHARACTERISTICS
OF THE COMMUNICATIVE ACT

Having seen in some detail a number of ways in which a society has had an impact upon its media, we need now turn our attention to the second of the basic questions with which social scientists approach the assessment of the communication revolution, namely, how does communication take place? Answers to this question are particularly important. A realistic assessment of a phenomenon such as mass communication can scarcely be achieved if there remain a number of controversies and unsettled issues concerning its basic nature. Unfortunately, this is precisely the situation with respect not only to *mass* communication, but to other forms of human communication as well.

The communication process is utterly fundamental to all of our psychological and social processes. Without repetitively engaging in acts of communication with our fellows, none of us could possibly develop the human mental processes and human social nature that distinguish us from other forms of life. Without language systems and other important tools of communication, we could not carry on the thousands of organized group processes that we use to coordinate our societal activities and lead our intensely interdependent lives. Yet in spite of the awesome importance of the communication process to every human being, every group, and every society, we know less about it than we do about the life cycle of the bat or the chemical composition of the sediment on the ocean floor.

Perhaps communication is too much a part of us even to study. It is so ubiquitous and pervasive that it seems like the air. You know it is there, but it is so available and so common that it does not seem terribly important to worry much about it. But worry about it we must, if we are to know *homo sapiens* better. If we are to unravel such mysteries as the basis of personality formation, the nature of mental illness, the sources of human conflict, and the principles of social change (to mention only a few), a more complete understanding of human communication is of paramount importance. This does not imply that the sole source of human difficulty or human achievement lies in communication. It is simply to suggest that such a wide variety of human problems in some way begin with the communication process that its nature urgently needs to be understood more adequately.

In spite of the fact that knowledge about communication has not accumulated in a manner commensurate with the importance of the problem, there are available the findings and conclusions of several disciplines that can offer a basis for beginning the task of developing a theory of the nature of human communication. The field of general semantics has yielded important insights into the nature of language and symbolic processes. Social psychology, especially the branch that focuses on symbolic interaction, has developed important propositions concerning the individual and communication. Learning theory, as developed by experimental psychologists, offers a number of leads to the nature of the acquisition, uses, and consequences of language. Other fields as well have made important contributions to an accumulating body of theory and research findings concerning different facets of communication. It is to these sources that we must turn in order to develop a theoretical analysis of the elementary characteristics of the communicative act. In the following sections, a number of propositions from a variety of fields are drawn together in an attempt to summarize not only the nature of communication, but some of its consequences for individuals and groups. No pretense is made that the resulting conceptual schemes are either sophisticated or particularly new. They will serve the purpose, however, of indicating about where we are now in the development of a general theory of communication. As will be quite clear, we really have not gotten very far.

COMMUNICATION PROCESSES
IN NONHUMAN ORGANISMS

One way of analyzing human communication is to contrast it with nonhuman communication. This, of course, implies that creatures other than man actually have the ability to communicate with each other. There are many living creatures, some far below man on the phylogenetic scale, that have the ability to influence their fellows and to be influenced by them in turn. This is not to say that such forms of communication proceed on the basis of exactly the same principles as communication in man. Nevertheless, what occurs between the so-called "social insects" as they carry out their highly organized group life or among a flock of migratory birds as they signal one another are forms of communication.

The social insects provide a convenient point of departure. Ants, bees, termites, and other insects exist together in colonies, often with an elaborate division of labor and a highly developed social organization by means of which they coordinate their activities and work toward their common goals.

Termites, like bees and ants, are social insects living in colonies. Like bees and ants, they work together, performing special tasks for the good of the colony, but, unlike them, they live together continuously, instead of interruptedly, in the nests or burrows. This colonial habit has given rise to different kinds of individuals or castes fitted structurally to perform definite functions in the life of the colony: soldiers for defense; a king and queen for reproduction, often replaced or supplemented by the supplemental reproductives; and usually a special caste called workers for the collection of food, the care of the king, queen, soldiers and young, and for the construction of the nest, burrows, exits, tunnels, towers, and exploratory extensions of the burrows.[1]

To maintain this organization, to carry out and coordinate the tasks that different individuals perform, some method of inter-individual exchange of influence is required. Insects of various types possess a variety of mechanisms by means of which they are able to influence each other's behavior. These mechanisms may be techniques for generating and receiving odors, sounds, tactile stimulation, or even visual stimuli. With the use of such techniques, fairly complex social activities can be coordinated as individual insects generate and receive stimuli from each other (Figure 6).

FIGURE 6. Communication Among Bees Through the Use of Patterned Movements

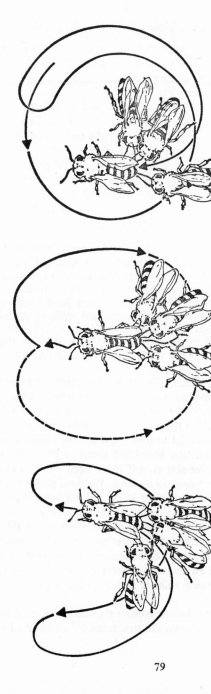

SICKLE DANCE is used by the Italian bee. She moves in a figure-eight-shaped pattern to show intermediate distance. A dancer is always followed by her hive-mates.

WAGGING DANCE indicates distance and direction of a nectar source farther away. Bee moves in a straight line, wagging her abdomen, then returns to her starting point.

ROUND DANCE, performed by moving in alternating circles to the left and to the right, is used by honeybees to indicate the presence of a nectar source near the hive.

Karl von Frisch, "Dialectics in the Language of Bees," *Scientific American*, Vol. 207, No. 2, August, 1962, pp. 78-87.

There is no reason to equate such behavior with the far more complex communication processes upon which human beings depend, but insect activities of this type can be recognized as a true form of communication—differing in principle from that of higher animal forms, but communication nevertheless. Insect communication is based exclusively upon inherited biological mechanisms. These can be very complex indeed, and many are as yet only poorly understood, but there is little doubt that whatever communication techniques an insect possesses were part of its genetic endowment. When appropriate stimuli are present in the environment, these communication techniques are triggered off automatically. The individual insect responds automatically to the communication signals of its own kind; this is not a process over which it has voluntary control.

Termites instinctively communicate with one another on contact in the burrow by means of their long sensitive antennae, which play rapidly over the surface of their neighbors. Alarm is also communicated throughout the colony by stridulating movements of the soldiers, feebly imitated by other members of the colony. The hard heads of the alarmed soldiers are rattled against the resonant walls of the narrow burrows, producing sounds which may be heard by applying one's ear closely to the surface of an infested post or pole. Rapping the pole sharply with a hammer will call forth these sounds of alarm.[2]

Communication among insects is for present purposes more interesting for what it is *not* than for what it is. It is an inherited, instinctual form of behavior, undoubtedly an end product of eons of adaptive evolution by means of which these relatively simple creatures maintain the social organization essential to their survival. Such communication does not involve learning. The individual insect is perfectly able to perform the communicative acts even if it has been raised in isolation and then returned to the colony as an adult. We need postulate neither conscious processes on the part of the individual nor cultural processes on the part of the colony. Once the biology of the insect becomes completely understood, the basis of the communicative act at this level of life will stand fully revealed. The assertion that insect communication does not involve learning, consciousness, or cultural processes implies that it is indeed an elementary form of communication compared to what occurs among animals higher on the phylogenetic continuum.

It is important to note, before leaving the communicating insects, that there is a close link between the structure of the individual organism and the communication process. In the case of the insects, this is an obvious and relatively simple relationship. The insect's biological structure determines the kinds of communicative acts he can perform. He can perform only those in his genetic repertoire, and he cannot help performing them upon receiving the appropriate stimuli. In other animal forms there are also important links between the communication process and individual structure. However, biological structure becomes somewhat less the rigid, limiting, and completely inflexible factor among higher animal forms than it is among bees, ants, termites, and other related insects. The learning process, at a minimum at the level of the insect, becomes increasingly important as one moves up the scale. The relationship between the organization of the individual and the communication process can still be said to exist, but it is not biological structure that is so important, but the *habit structure* the individual acquires as a product of learning.

To illustrate how communication takes place among animals higher on the evolutionary continuum than insects, but lower than man, and to show the relationship between this process and the habit organization of the individual, we may turn to the so-called "pecking order" among hens. This interesting phenomenon is simply the organization or pattern of dominance and submission that develops between the individual members of a newly formed flock of hens when they are kept for some time in the same pen or confined area. In any given pair, the dominant hen pecks the submissive one, but not vice versa. An elaborate hierarchy is eventually worked out, with a particular hen at the top, able to dominate all others, and with the more submissive hens near the bottom, dominated by those above. This particular type of social organization is widely found among animals, where patterns of dominance and submission are established and continuously reinforced by various techniques. The relationship between this process and the communicative act is that some form of communication is essential to maintain the social organization, once it has been worked out. Also, the position of the individual within this pattern is largely a product of his communicative experiences within the structure. Thus, both social organization and individual organization of response patterns are closely linked to the communication process as it is carried on within such a setting.

We will show clearly that the individual's position in the pecking order, and his techniques for helping maintain it, are *learned* and not inherited. Yet, the pecking order is by no means completely independent of biological factors. Experiments have shown that hens injected with male hormones will be more aggressive and will fight their way up higher in the structure. Similarly, large doses of female hormones will make the hen more submissive and it will suffer a consequent loss of position. The pecking orders are also sex-bound. That is, roosters peck each other but do not peck hens. Hens establish their own order and do not challenge the roosters. In a mixed flock there will be two such hierarchies. In short, such biological factors as hormone balance, sex category, strength, and of course general anatomical structure operate as prerequisite and limiting factors in helping determine the place of a given individual within the social structure which is eventually worked out. At the same time, the pecking order is not simply a product of inheritance, and it can be quickly forgotten:

A chicken's memory is short. Hens that have been separated for two weeks or more will fight the battle for dominance all over again when they are brought together. If a strange bird enters an organized flock, it has to fight each of the residents to establish its status.[3]

But what does this all have to do with communication? The phenomenon of the pecking order, and indeed the act of pecking itself is a classic illustration of a particular *type* of communication, namely communication based upon the *natural sign*. To explain the implications of this assertion, consider the following simplified explanation of how the act of pecking becomes established and how it operates as a means of communication:

When adult chickens that have not previously been together are placed as a group into a pen, they engage in a series of combats by pairs. Each chicken will pair off against one opponent at a time, until eventually the order of dominance is established. A given pair may have to fight it out several times before the final outcome is clear and the dominance-submission issue is settled. Finally, the dominant chicken is able to signal to the submissive one his higher position by simply delivering a peck. The simple peck has in some way become a *substitute* for the elaborate series of acts that make up a complete beating given to another chicken. Similarly, the slight gesture of submission on the part of the recipient of the peck has become a substitute for the complete act of getting beaten by and eventually submitting to the more aggressive chicken. In some manner, these simplified and much truncated acts come to "stand for" the more dramatic, complicated, and extended series of behaviors associated with victory and defeat in combat.

FIGURE 7. Forming the Pecking Order Among Chickens

The pecking order position of a given chicken results from a series of individual combats among the members of a newly established flock. This drawing depicts two Rhode Island Red pullets fighting to determine dominance and submission.

A. M. Guhl, "The Social Order of Chickens," *Scientific American*, Vol. 194, No. 2, February, 1956, pp. 42-47.

Whenever a beginning portion of an act or series of acts, or some other portion or limited segment of the series, becomes capable of arousing the same internal responses that were previously aroused only by the entire act or series of acts, we are confronted with an example of a *gesture.* Just as the clenched fist shaken in the face of the opponent arouses in him the response of a potential blow which could follow, or one which perhaps did once occur, the peck arouses for the chicken the inner response that was formerly aroused by his part of the combat. This substitution of a limited segment of the act for the whole complex act or series of acts is a natural product of learning for the chicken. The peck is a *natural sign* for each of the chickens of the events of the more extended action series. Gestures are one type of natural sign when they occur in this way among animals. Such gestures really should not be confused with those used by human beings, and the example of the clenched fist was not directly comparable. The reason for this is that we need not assume that the chickens have any cognitive processes related to the use of such signs. Although the peck as a means of communicating dominance and submission is a product of learning, it may be in every way nearly as automatic as is the initiation of a sound signal by an insect under appropriate stimulus conditions or response to such a sound by another insect. We need not assume that the dominant hen says to itself, "I think I'll peck that other chicken to show who's boss," or that the other chicken upon seeing the first chicken advance says internally, "Oh-oh, here it comes again; I might as well submit." The exchange of influence on each other's behavior is simply a product of *conditioned responses* that have emerged from the positive and negative reinforcements of the combat situation.

The conclusion that pecks are learned sign substitutes for more complex forms of behavior is well supported by an additional characteristic of the dominance-submission behavior among chickens. Eventually, they even substitute a simpler act for the peck itself:

Once the peck order has been determined, pecking begins to decline in frequency as members of the hierarchy recognize their superiors; eventually a mere *raising or lowering of the head* [italics supplied] may be enough to signify dominance or submission respectively.[4]

Thus it is that the beginning phase of the pecking act begins to serve as a natural sign for the entire act. This new and much simplified gesture then becomes the means of communication the flock uses to maintain and reinforce its social organization when it has become deeply institutionalized.

The communication patterns among chickens, like those among termites, are interesting primarily as a contrasting framework against which human communication can be compared. Termite communication and chicken communication illustrate how creatures very different from man are able to influence and coordinate each other's conduct. While biological factors alone are sufficient to account for communication among the social insects, and biological factors plus reinforcement learning of individual habit patterns are enough to explain communication among more advanced forms of animal life, these factors cannot fully account for the incredible complexity of communication among human beings. But before discussing human communication in depth, several additional issues need clarification.

We noted that the communicative act among animals capable of learning is based upon the natural sign. The essence of a natural sign is that it is a new stimulus preceding another stimulus (capable of calling out some response) in time in such a way that after a limited number of occurrences of an appropriate sequence the new stimulus becomes capable of calling out the response, by-passing the original stimulus, and thus forming in the individual a new habit. There is no assumption that the individual organism learning to respond to a natural sign is capable of voluntarily initiating the sign itself. If the natural sign happens to be a gesture that is initiated by one organism and serves as a stimulus for another organism, it is assumed that the initiator simply makes the gesture as a normal response to whatever environmental stimuli are present to which its behavior has become linked through learning. Only when two organisms have individually developed a set of learned habit patterns that *happen to be coordinated,* so that a response from one can serve as a stimulus to the other, can communication of this type take place. However, this type of communication is common in nature. It is widely found among mammals, birds, fish, and other animals that normally travel or exist in some sort of band, flock, or grouping.

Communication of this type is automatic, requires no assumptions of consciousness or cognitive functioning on the part of either organism. Furthermore, there is no assumption that whatever movement or act is used as a signal is assigned *arbitrarily* as a substitute for the more extended series of acts (combat, flight, etc.). One of the chickens in our example could not arbitrarily decide to let a wiggle of the claw or a flip of the tail be the substitute stimulus signifying dominance or submission rather than the peck. Neither do they mutually agree in any sense that the appropriate response to a peck will be to make a minor submissive gesture on the part of those who have been defeated in combat. They are simply incapable of establishing any such *conventions* among them. The peck becomes a sign because it occurs quite naturally at the appropriate point in the chicken's repertoire. The same is true of the submissive gesture. In short, the relationship between the sign (substitute stimulus) and its referent (that for which it is a substitute) is neither arbitrary nor conventional. It is part of the specific habit structure of the individual. It may or may not have a parallel in the specific habit structure of other individuals with which the animal associates. If such counterpart stimulus-response relationships exist for two or more organisms, these constitute a basis for the communicative act—they permit mutual influence on conduct and even possible coordination of activities.

Coordination of activities can take place only if the responses each animal makes internally to the particular sign used in communication are mutually coordinated. Thus, if the truncated act of raising the head arouses in the dominant chicken the internal feeling of engaging in and winning a combat, and if the sight of this stimulus arouses in the submissive chicken the internal experience of having fought but been defeated, then there can be the coordinated mutual influence that we have identified as one type of communication. In a very restricted sense, the internal learned responses thus aroused in the animals can be called "meanings." We must note immediately, however, that each chicken in the exchange has a "meaning" which is unique to it, a product of its particular experience that is quite different from the internal meaning response of the other animal. That is, there is no *shared* meaning, no isomorphism, no identity of form between the structure of the internal responses aroused by the act for the dominant chicken as compared to the submissive one. (It is on this point in particular that substantial differences exist between communication occurring among animals and among human beings.)

The usage of the term "meaning," which is implied in the above analysis, may seem unusual to the reader accustomed to think of this term in more complex ways. However, defined in this way, the concept of meaning is simply the internal experiences animals have in connection with particular stimuli that impinge upon their perceptual processes. If stable habit patterns are connected with such stimuli in such a way that they arouse internal responses of the type that only the actual object or event originally aroused, this constitutes sign behavior. If the sign behaviors of two animals are coordinated adequately (as in the example of the chickens), then communication of a particular type can take place. We can, of course, never directly observe such inner experiences and must make inferences about them. Such inferred constructs are widely used in science.

THE NATURE AND SIGNIFICANCE
OF HUMAN COMMUNICATION

As is the case among animals, human communication involves biological structure. Before a given individual can adequately learn the complex habit patterns involved in the use of language, he must have a neural structure which functions within the normal range. Similarly, insofar as the various senses and the musculature are involved in speaking, hearing, and seeing during the communicative act among human beings, it has biological components. These components serve as prerequisite conditions rather than causal factors. In addition, the individual human being must undergo a long period of learning before he develops habit patterns, which permit him to respond to particular gestures, verbal and other, as substitute signs that have as their referents objects and events in the world of reality. The human communicative act shares these characteristics with the communicative act as it exists among other animal forms capable of sign learning. However, it is at this point that the similarity ends.

Unlike the animal, the human being is born into an ongoing and elaborate culture. An important feature of this culture is the set of *conventions* which exist concerning the relationship between signs and their referents. For any given language (set of signs), the connection between a particular word of the language and that for which the word is a substitute is both arbitrary and conventional. In the historical development of language, particular objects or events were signified by specific sound patterns. These assignments were at first arbitrary. For example, the word "beatnik" did not exist in the English language prior to the post-World War II period, when the formation of groups with particular social protests occurred. No one is sure how this arbitrary assignment came about, but it was somehow established. Once established, however, this particular vocal gesture began to serve as a substitute stimulus, that is a sign, for which the referent was a particular type of deviant individual. As usage persisted, it became conventional. That is, there developed an institutionalized practice to respond to this particular noise by internally experiencing objects of this type. The existence of an established set of conventions, concerning the referents of gestures which originally may have been arbitrarily assigned, gives the human being an enormous advantage over other animal forms. We may designate a sign or gesture that is both arbitrary and conventional in the sense outlined above as a *symbol*. Many kinds of symbols exist.

A list of examples would be extensive, ranging through military insignia, sorority emblems, Morse code, algebraic symbols, and hundreds more. The most common, of course, are language symbols, verbal or written. Like all symbols, these are signs (substitute stimuli) that have as their referents events, things, or other phenomena, for which the verbal noise or written mark is a convenient substitute. Once learned, these convenient substitutes arouse the "meaning" responses in the individual that only the referent itself originally aroused. While many animals acquire the ability to respond to (have meanings for) signs, only human beings can use symbols. The entire range of symbols (words and otherwise) used by a given society constitutes its language.

We have, to be sure, left unanswered important questions concerning the origins of language, the source of arbitrary assignments, conventions, etc. However, these are beyond the scope of the present analysis. We may take the existence of language as given, recognizing that its slow development over eons of time is as yet ill understood. But the important thing is that the human being is born into an existing learning environment where language is conspicuously present. This happy circumstance makes it possible for him to acquire tools for communication with his fellows that are considerably more complex than those of his nearest animal neighbors.

As the individual slowly acquires, during his infancy and childhood, the ability to respond in conventionalized ways to the vocal and written symbols that constitute his language, he is developing a repertoire of *meanings* in much the same sense as was implied by this term in earlier paragraphs of the present chapter. That is, "meaning" is a product of learning. A person's meaning for a particular symbol is the set of responses that the individual learns to make to it. At first, he can have such an internal experience only to the referent object or event itself, as a baby experiences painful heat when exposed to the stimulus of a boiling teakettle, a match, an oven, etc. Upon repeatedly undergoing this experience, however, following the warning utterance of mother that the object is "hot," he soon learns to have much the same internal experience to the vocal noise "hot" as he did earlier to the original objects that aroused the painful experience itself. Once such a habit has been established, he can respond to this particular verbal symbol by undergoing the corresponding internal experience even in the absence of high temperature objects. However, only insofar as his habitual responses to the symbol more or less parallel those of others and insofar as he understands that this is the case, can such a symbol be used in the human communicative act.

Once such a conventionalized "meaning" has become part of his repertoire, he can learn to *initiate* this particular vocal gesture (symbol) himself, and respond to it in much the same way as he did earlier when it was initiated by someone else. This ability to initiate symbols and to respond to them oneself in conventionalized ways is very definitely a uniquely human accomplishment. It is undoubtedly a product of two factors, the enormous learning capacity of the average human being, and the prior existence of the cultural conventions of language.

The ability the human being has to initiate particular verbal gestures (words), which have associated with them conventionalized referents and internal meaning responses, and to respond to these symbols in much the same ways that other individuals (who share the conventions) respond, is of course the ability to engage in human thought! The internal manipulation of meaning—the mental functioning of the human individual—then, is critically linked to his involvement in a conventionalized language process, as George Herbert Mead so aptly pointed out several decades ago.[5]

Not only does the participation of the individual in the language process provide him with the means to communicate with himself (think); it provides him with the ability to communicate with his fellows through conventionalized meanings. If the individual has learned to initiate a symbol that he responds to himself in the same way that he knows others will respond, he has acquired the technique of human communication. In fact, the communicative act at the level of the human being involves exactly these elements. Where in the case of animals, communication proceeded on the basis of coordinated but *unlike* internal meanings for natural signs, man's communication takes place because of isomorphism, that is, a certain *identity* between the internal meaning responses that separate individuals have learned to make toward a given symbol. A symbol that arouses the same general set of internal responses (meanings) within the individual initiating the stimulus as are aroused within the individual who perceives the stimulus is called a *significant symbol*. It is through the significant symbol that the human being learns to manipulate meanings within himself (thought) and in exchanges with others (interpersonal communication). Such symbolic interaction sharply separates the human being from other animals.

Much has been made of the symbolic interaction process. The nature and structure of the language and the symbolic habits and significant symbols of a given people provide important keys to their social organization. Individual personality formation is also in large part a product of the communicative exchanges that the individual has engaged in.[6]

It is no exaggeration to say that the human communicative act, proceeding on the basis of the significant symbol, is a prerequisite ability without which it would not be possible for man to have developed his societies and cultures to the elaborate degree that he has. In fact, it is not possible to imagine any form of human society that could exist without this facility. The communicative act is the means by which a group's norms are expressed, by means of which social control is exerted, roles are allocated, coordination of effort is achieved, expectations are made manifest, and the entire social process is carried on. Without such exchanges of influence human society would simply collapse.

It is equally true that the involvement of the individual in the community of language is the key to his psychological nature. Without learning to use symbols and their associated internal meanings, he would be unable to manipulate meanings, form beliefs about himself, ponder a problem, have human emotions, grasp a principle, plan ahead, learn in retrospect from the lessons of the past, and perform other human acts. He would be about at the level of an intelligent chicken or at best at the level of a super-ape. He would be able to acquire unique meaning responses to natural signs, and if these happened to interlock with different meanings that other individuals had acquired to the same signs, some limited coordination of behavior could take place. But his mind and his conception of himself and his society would remain at the animal level.

It is thus that the arbitrary and conventionalized sign—the significant symbol—is the element which sharply distinguishes man from other forms of life.

HUMAN SYSTEMS FOR ACHIEVING ISOMORPHISM IN MEANING

But how does the human being use this unique facility to carry out the communicative act? We know that the significant symbol is the key element distinguishing man from other creatures; but how does this element operate in the communicative exchange that results in one individual understanding the initiated communication stimuli of another? To answer this question, we need to develop a theoretical construct, an abstract model of the system within which the communicative act takes place. If the construct is made sufficiently general, it can encompass *mass* communication as well as more simple interpersonal communication.

The problem of communication is not actually a "transfer" of meaning. In the communicative act, there is no essence, spirit, or invisible "something" that leaves the central nervous system of one person and travels to that of another. Such a concept is unnecessary and muddies the water of legitimate inquiry into the nature of human communication with questions about "thought transference," "clairvoyance," "mind reading" and other such inanities.

But if the communicative act is not a "transfer" of meaning, then how does communication occur? A convenient way of answering this question is that it takes place through the operation of a particular set of components in a theoretical system, the consequence of which is that there is *isomorphism* between the internal responses (meanings) to a given set of symbols on the part of both sender and receiver. Many attempts have been made to conceptualize the theoretical system that is basic to the communication process. The system analyzed in the paragraphs below makes no claim of being original. It is an extension of the ideas of a number of previous writers.[7] It does show, however, how the use of the significant symbol makes possible the achievement of a certain identity of meaning between a communicator and the person or persons toward whom he addresses his messages.

Figure 8 presents in schematic form the basic components of a theoretical system for the achievement of isomorphism of meaning between individuals engaged in the communicative act, that is, for "getting the meaning coordinated" between communicator and audience. The first general component in this system is a *source*. It is the function of the source to formulate "meaning" into "message." That is, to select appropriate significant symbols (message) with which to express the internal responses (meanings) the communicator wishes to present to his audience. The transformation of meaning to message makes the former externally available in the form of significant symbols. In the case of a two-person communication system, the source would be the individual person's cognitive processes, what he uses to experience the internal responses we have called meaning.[8] In the case of mass communication, the source might be some organized group that has formulated its collective meanings into some message the group as a whole wishes to convey through a single spokesman.

The second component in the abstract scheme is the *transmitter*. Its function is to encode—to transform the "message" into "information." Information will be defined as some type of event in the physical

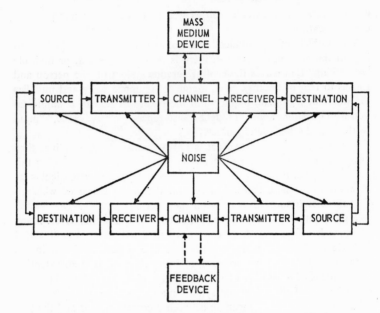

FIGURE 8. The Components of a General System for Achieving Isomorphism of Meaning

world which will permit movement over space. Electrical impulses
traveling along a wire, electromagnetic radiations in the air, printed
visual stimuli on paper, and agitations of the air molecules are all
examples of "information." It is these events in the physical world that
conquer distance between distinct individuals and not some mysterious
movement of meaning from the mind of one person to that of another.

Generally speaking, source and transmitter are but different phases
of the communicative act carried out by the originator of the communication. They are analytically separable functions of the single
human being. When a person talks, he selects symbols to express his
denotative and connotative meanings (formulates meaning into message) and then enunciates verbally or writes these symbols (encodes
message to information) in such a way that they are converted into
either auditory or visual events that can be perceived as stimuli by his
audience.

A third component in this system is some form of *channel*. In the case of one person talking to another, this is simply the air through which information (agitations of the air molecules) moves. For techniques of communication other than verbal, e.g., written, telegraphic, etc., other types of channels would move the information across space. Mass communication requires more complex channels, which will be discussed below.

Linked with the channel in this system is the *receiver*. This component has the function of receiving the information and "decoding" it—transforming the physical events of the information back into a message (system of significant symbols). In the case of ordinary talking, this would be done by the auditory apparatus of the human being, receiving air vibrations and transforming them into neural impulses, so they can become recognizable verbal symbols. In the case of written communication, visual mechanisms would perform parallel functions.

Once the message (set of symbols) has been perceived, the final component, namely the *destination,* responds to these with the denotative and connotative internal experiences we are calling meaning. Thus, the function of the destination is to interpret "message" into "meaning."

After these components have functioned, if the meaning of the destination is isomorphic with the meaning of the source which originated the act, then communication can be said to have taken place. Thus, communication amounts to achieving a parallel in the structure of the internal meaning responses of both a source and a destination. The meanings remain in the behavioral systems (cognitive structures) of the respective parties, and it is their similarity that constitutes communication and not their "movement."

Obviously, the achievement of perfect correspondence between every element of the denotative and connotative meaning responses of both source and destination is seldom achieved, because human communication is almost always in some degree less than perfect. There are a number of reasons for this, some psychological, some cultural, and some simply mechanical.[9] But whatever the source of this lack of isomorphism of meanings, the degree to which they are less than absolutely identical, element for element, can be called *noise*. This may be an undesirable feature of the communication system, but nonetheless, it is almost always present. For this reason, *noise* must be recognized as an additional component of the theoretical system of the communicative act. Its function (consequence) is to reduce to some degree the correspondence between the pattern of response elements constituting the meaning of the source and the counterpart meaning of the destination.

To this set of theoretical components, which function between source and destination, we need add another set functioning in the other direction. Nearly always, when one individual engages in the communicative act with another, there is some sort of perceptible feedback originating in the communicatee which the communicator uses as data for modifying his message. For example, if the communicatee winces, grins, raises an eyebrow, or just looks blank as the communicator enunciates his words, this constitutes a kind of message returning to the communicator. He may choose to illustrate further, use a less complex vocabulary, or otherwise alter his presentation because of this feedback. In short, during the communicative act, the destination also operates as a source of feedback and the source as destination for feedback messages. Whether this feedback is unwitting, in the form of culturally defined gestures, for example the raised eyebrow, or is given in carefully chosen significant symbols is unimportant for our theoretical analysis. It simply implies that the system we are developing does require a reverse set of components.

The reverse components are also afflicted by noise. Gestures can be misunderstood, facial expressions or other data can be misinterpreted just as words can be incorrectly understood. A classic example is the case of Abraham Lincoln, whose audience failed to cheer or applaud after his Gettysburg address. He concluded that it had been an inadequate speech, while his audience was actually so moved by it that they felt applause would have been inappropriate.

This two-way set of components operates as a system, then, with information moving first one way and then another, or both ways at the same time. It can operate with extreme rapidity in an ongoing conversation, or more slowly if the two parties are using written or other forms of communication.

To accommodate the mass communication process, this elementary theoretical system must be somewhat elaborated. Essentially, this is an elaboration of the *channel* in both the major and the feedback set of components. The channel conveys information to some mechanical device, such as a radio broadcasting transmitter, which is essentially a process for transforming one kind of information into another which is somewhat more effective in spanning distance. The speaker's voice causes air vibrations (information) that are transformed into another form of information (electric impulses) and are further transformed into electromagnetic waves. These in turn are picked up by the home radio set, transformed back into electrical impulses, and converted back into agitations of the air. Parallel accounts can easily be constructed for the words of the newspaper reporter, who first places his message on his typewriter by the hunt-and-peck system. These are then set into linotype, sent to the press, delivered to the home, etc., by an elaborate process that substantially multiplies the number of persons who can be exposed at a given time to his messages. These elaborations are additional complexities of detail, however, and do not alter the communicative act in principle. The reporter is still the source and transmitter that converts meanings to information. Any given reader is still a receiver and destination which decodes visual information to message and responds to the stimuli with meaning responses. The fact that the channel has become considerably elaborated does not change the fundamental characteristics of this communicative act. There also is a clear feedback set of components, although the details of these are likely to vary considerably from one mass medium to another. Letters to the editor are different in detail from the results of an audience rating system, where a sample of the audience can give its preference rankings for given television programs. In spite of these differences of technique, there are still the components of source, noise, destination, etc.

It is also true that mass communication is likely to involve large numbers of people in addition to complex mechanical or electronic elaborations of the channels. However, this is a difference of quantity rather than of principle. The relationship between a given mass communicator and a given member of his audience still takes place with significant symbols; the nature of meaning remains the same; and the communicative act still occurs through the various components that have been outlined above.

While these differences between mass communication and simpler forms of interpersonal communication do not involve differences in fundamental principles, this does not mean that they are unimportant. The degree to which isomorphism of meaning or perhaps to which overt compliance to messages occurs when a given communication involves a mass medium as compared to direct face-to-face communication is a proper object of research. There is a voluminous literature which suggests that such differences do occur, and for this reason, mass communication can differ considerably in its *consequences*—its effect on conduct as compared to communication by other means. While the communicative act follows the same theoretical principles in all forms of human communication, the consequences of the act may differ substantially as different techniques for moving information are employed.

Having seen something of the underlying principles that occur in human communication, mass and otherwise, we need next to ask how the communicative act can have some impact upon the individuals who engage in it. In particular, how does mass communication influence the audiences of the media? As will be seen in the next chapter, the answer to this question involves some of the most complex theories of the social and behavioral sciences.

Chapter VI

MASS SOCIETY
AND THE MASS MEDIA

To TRY to explain the consequences of the mass media of communication for the audiences whose attentions are turned toward them, a wide variety of ideas, assumptions, theories, and hypotheses has been advanced over a considerable number of years. In their theoretical thinking about the impact of the mass media of communication, scholars, critics, and enthusiasts have all been influenced in greater or lesser degree by the conceptions of the fundamental nature of man and his society that have been current in their time. Such conceptions of the social order and of individual psychological organization have undergone considerable change during the century that saw the rise of the media. An increasingly pressing need rose to understand how they operate within that social order and the manner in which they influence individual members of society as well as the social process. Although the lines of influence between general behavioral science theory and conceptualizations of the mass communication process have by no means been perfectly clear, it is important to show some of the ways in which students of communication have been influenced by general theorists. This can clarify in part why media scholars, or others who have commented on the nature of the mass communication process, have come up with the particular notions that they have. Effective contributions to mass communication theory have been made by the various behavioral sciences. However, the present chapter will treat in somewhat greater detail those from some of the earlier sociological theories of the general nature of society. This is not to minimize other contributions; our purpose is to give a reasonably detailed account of the historical influence of sociologists on mass communication theory.

The task of showing these lines of influence involves two basic difficulties. First, theories of the nature of society have never been uniform at any given point in time. In fact, sociologists of different theoretical persuasions have seen the organization of societal processes and changing patterns in societal relations from very different perspectives all through the history of sociological thought. Theories of society in the 19th century were developed on the basis of complex organic models. Later, the rise of quantitative research procedures introduced new ideas that substantially influenced the analysis of the nature of society and brought additional schisms into sociological theory. More recently, the introduction of "functionalism" and the growth of interest in "social systems" has produced still further divisions, but it has tended to return the thinking of many theorists to organic type conceptualizations. Secondly, on the other side of the coin, there have really never been any rigorously articulated sets of theories concerning mass communication. As we shall see even at the present time, there is no body of relatively consistent, agreed upon, and formalized assertions that can truly be called "mass communication theory." To be sure, there has been a great deal of speculation about the way in which mass communication takes place; much energy has been spent on charges and countercharges concerning the manner in which the media may influence individuals and groups; and from time to time various conceptual schemes or even broad hypotheses have been widely discussed with respect to some phase of mass communication or some aspect of the media. There has also been a substantial accumulation of empirical data that illuminates particular communication processes or specific effects. But as yet, even though we use the phrase "mass communication theory," the field has not been unified by the development of a standard set of concepts, an interrelated body of hypotheses, or an overall explanatory framework. In fact, it is fair to say that there is no real agreement in this interdisciplinary area of study as to exactly what constitutes the subject matter of the field of "mass communication." One contemporary writer has even proclaimed the field to be dead.[1] About the best one can do is to reconstruct in retrospect the types of theoretical assumptions that seem to underly the analyses of problems associated with mass communication at particular times.

Given the above-mentioned lack of coordination, the task of tracing relationships between general thought concerning the nature of society and more specific interpretations of the nature and effects of mass communication may seem hopeless. Yet, it is a necessary task; thinking about mass communication has changed, and this change has not been random. There has been something like a progressive development and increasing sophistication of ideas concerning the media and their impact, in spite of the fact that this development has often been, and remains, halting and disorderly. Clearly, we now know more about mass communication than we did in 1920; we also know more about it than we did in 1940 or even 1960. But, we must account for the direction of this change and formulate some idea of where it has led us. Only when we understand clearly what have been the underlying postulates concerning the nature of societal processes in general can we begin to understand why hypotheses related to mass communication have been formulated in the way they have. The importance of establishing such linkages between general theory and mass communication theory is not so much that we may more clearly view in retrospect the factors that have influenced thinking about the media in the past, but that we may formulate more adequate theories in the future and fully understand their bases. With this perspective in mind, we turn to an overview of sociological thought insofar as it has influenced students of the mass media during the early part of the communication revolution.

THE RISE OF THE IMAGE OF THE MASS SOCIETY

Society is large and organized. It also seems to grow more complex. These two elementary observations were the foundations upon which the systems of thought of the founding fathers of sociology were developed. Speculation about the nature of the social order—the manner in which it is changing or how it might be improved—had been the subject of philosophical writing since the beginning of recorded human experience. However, the founding of sociology as a systematic discipline devoted specifically to the study of societal processes did not take place until the first half of the 19th century, at about the same time that Benjamin Day started selling his newspaper on the streets of New York for a penny a copy.

Auguste Comte is usually credited with giving the new field its name, and he also advocated the application of the Positive (Scientific) Method to the study of society. Comte's major contributions to the task of studying social phenomena scientifically were more philosophical than substantive. However, he did include in his voluminous writings an *organic conception of society,* a theoretical model that was widely used by pioneer sociologists.

The concept of society as organism was not original with Comte, but he made it a fundamental postulate. The significance of this idea is that important consequences follow from it. In simple terms, society can be thought of as a particular type of organism, namely a *collective organism.* This did not mean for Comte that there is just a rough analogy between the organization of some individual biological organism, such as a particular plant or animal, and a human society. Comte assumed that society was an organism in its own right. He saw that it had structure, that specialized parts functioned together, that the whole was something more than the sum of its parts, and that it underwent evolutionary change. These characteristics were those of organisms in general, and so society could be properly classified as such, recognizing that it clearly differed from other specific varieties of organisms.

Comte marveled at the great diversity of tasks, goals, and functions that characterized a society and commented on how each individual and group can seem to be pursuing private ends and yet the overall result is that of a harmoniously functioning system. One of the basic principles of the organization of society (as organism) which accounts for this interested him greatly. That principle was *specialization.* The division of functions that men voluntarily assume, he felt, was the key not only to the continued stability of society, but also to its possible disorganization.

The main cause of the superiority of the social to the individual organism is, according to an established law, the more marked specialty of the various functions fulfilled by organs more and more distinct, but interconnected; so that the unity of aim is more and more combined with diversity of means. We cannot, of course, fully appreciate a phenomenon which is forever proceeding before our eyes, and in which we bear a part; but if we withdraw ourselves in thought from the social system, and contemplate it as from afar, can we conceive of a more marvellous spectacle, in the whole range of natural phenomena, than the regular and constant convergence of an innumerable multitude of human beings, each possessing a distinct and, in a certain degree, independent existence, and yet incessantly disposed, amidst all their discordance of talent and character, to concur in many ways in the same general development, without concert, and even consciousness on the part of most of them, who believe that they are merely following their personal impulses? . . . This reconciliation of the individuality of labour with cooperation of endeavors, which becomes more remarkable as society grows more complex and extended, constitutes the radical character of human operations [at the societal level].[2]

Comte saw great harmony and stability, then, arising from the assumption of specialized functions by individuals. He felt that inevitably these specialized activities would all contribute to the general equilibrium of society in that, "... all individual organizations, even the most vicious and imperfect (short of monstrosity), may finally be made use of for the general good."[3]

But Comte also saw danger in too much specialization. It should be added that this point is of considerable significance for the student of mass communication, because the same idea was used by later theorists to develop the concept of the *mass society*. The mass society concept was of central importance for early thinking about the media. The most important element of this idea was that ineffective social organization failed to provide adequate linkages between individuals to maintain an integrated and stable system of social control. This theme is clearly stated by Comte:

Some economists have pointed out, but in a very inadequate way, the evils of an exaggerated division of material labour, and I have indicated, in regard to the more important field of scientific labour, the mischievous intellectual consequences of the spirit of specialty which at present prevails. It is necessary to estimate directly the principle of such an influence, in order to understand the object of the spontaneous system of requisites for the continuous preservation of society. In decomposing, we always disperse; and the distribution of human labours must occasion individual divergencies, both intellectual and moral, which require a permanent discipline to keep them within bounds. If the separation of the social functions develops a useful spirit of detail, on the one hand, it tends, on the other, to extinguish or restrict what we call the aggregate or general spirit.[4]

Comte went on to discuss extensively and critically the possible consequences of an overexpansion of the division of labor. He felt that the more individuals were unlike each other in their position in the social system, the greater would be their reduction of understanding of their fellow citizens. He saw that people with the same specialty would develop ties with each other, but would become alienated from other such groupings. "Thus it is that the principle by which alone general society could be developed and extended, threatens, in another view, to decompose it into a multitude of unconnected corporations, which almost seem not to belong to the same species. ..."[5]

As the societal organism evolves (according to this type of theory), it develops harmony and stability through its division of labor. At the same time, there is the possibility that overdevelopment can lead to disorganization and decline by disrupting the basis for effective communication between individual parts of the organism. Given the postulate of the organic nature of society, the concept of specialization of function follows by definition. But an increasing degree of such specialization leads to increased social differentiation. If such differentiation reaches the point where effective linkages between parts of the system are threatened, then the equilibrium and harmony of the organism is also threatened. This theme recurs in the writings of later theorists, and is one of the basic beginning points for discussing "mass" society. The relationship between this idea and "mass" communication will be made clear.

It should be recalled that Comte worked out his views of the nature of society during the 1830's. This was before the industrial revolution had achieved a wide impact on Europe. Comte felt somewhat threatened by the possibility of an increasing level of specialization in the society he saw before him. But social theorists who came later were confronted with the *reality* of a great increase in the division of labor which the new industrialization was bringing. It is little wonder they were deeply impressed with its implications.

Speculation about the organic nature of society and its consequences constituted only a minor part of the work of Comte. However, the second founder of modern sociology, Herbert Spencer, pursued the organic concept with great vigor and in great depth. Spencer, like Comte, was primarily a philosopher and was concerned about science as a means for obtaining valid knowledge. This concern led him to formulate what he thought were the most important principles that seemed to him to pervade all the sciences. His famous *laws of evolution* (from which Darwin drew inspiration) were given complete development in his work, *First Principles*, published in 1863, more than twenty years after Comte had completed his *Positive Philosophy*.

Spencer applied his evolutionary concepts to the study of society and wrote *The Principles of Sociology* in four volumes between 1876 and 1896. There are many parallels between the two writers, but Spencer claims that his own ideas were worked out independently of those of Comte. In any case, the theory of society which Spencer elaborated in great detail was a purely organic one. After defining society as a functioning system, he discussed the social order at length in terms of its growth, structures, functions, systems of organs, etc., developing an extremely elaborate (outright) analogy between society and an individual organism.

The division of labor was a very important part of this analysis, and was regarded as the basic unifying factor which held the organism together:

The division of labour, first dwelt upon by political economists as a social phenomenon, and thereupon recognized by biologists as a phenomenon of living bodies, which they called the "physiological division of labour," is that which in the society, as in the animal, makes it a living whole. Scarcely can I emphasize enough the truth that in respect of this fundamental trait, a social organism and an individual organism are entirely alike. . . .

[Society] undergoes continuous growth. As it grows, its parts become unlike: it exhibits increase of structure. The unlike parts simultaneously assume activities of unlike kinds. These activities are not simply different, but their differences are so related as to make one another possible. The reciprocal aid thus given causes mutual dependence of the parts. And the mutually-dependent parts, living by and for one another, form an aggregate constituted on the same general principle as an individual organism.[6]

But Spencer did not go to the next step and contemplate the possible *difficulties* for society that might occur if specialization went too far. He was convinced that the most fundamental process of nature was evolution, and that evolution was natural and therefore good. The great changes that he observed in English society, as the industrial order came, he regarded as an unfolding of society according to natural evolutionary laws. To suggest that social changes brought by natural evolution might be undesirable was unthinkable. So deeply did he hold these views that he became convinced that any interference in the natural development of society was completely unwarranted and was bound to have disastrous consequences. He bitterly opposed legislation aimed at any form of social improvement on the grounds that nature meant the fittest to survive, and in the long run this would benefit society. While Comte advocated planned social change, Spencer argued vigorously for a policy of almost complete *laissez faire*.

Even so, it can be seen that the two major founders of sociology developed similar organic evolutionary models of the social order and both postulated a process leading to increasing social differentiation. The one had grave reservations as to the possible consequences of over-specialization, and the other had grave reservations over any attempt to interfere in what he regarded as the natural evolution of the society. Neither had any full appreciation of the fundamental changes in the structure of the social order that were to come with the 20th century. Comte, writing on the eve of the industrial revolution, and Spencer, writing during its early phases, could not foresee that the very fabric of society would be changed by the upheaval in the economic institution that the factory system and the new economic order would bring. The same acceleration in science that brought the mass media of communication, and indeed that prompted these two philosophers to found a science of society, also fashioned the forces of society's new industrial organization. The impact of this new order was to be felt in every corner of the world.

Another theoretical formulation came from the province of Schleswig-Holstein in Germany. In 1887, a young man of that region by the name of Ferdinand Tönnies produced a theoretical sociological analysis entitled *Gemeinschaft und Gesellschaft*. In this work, he posed two contrasting theoretical types of societal organization—one preindustrial and the other largely a product of industrialization. In his analysis of the nature of society, Tönnies concentrated less upon organic analogies, or the possible consequences of specialization, but focused his attention upon the kinds of social bonds that exist between the members of societies and groups in two very distinct types of social organization.

Gemeinschaft does not translate easily into English. The word "community" is often offered as its equivalent, but the complexity of Tönnies' meaning is not well captured by such a simple translation. The idea of Gemeinschaft is best illustrated by suggesting some of the kinds of interpersonal ties that are included within it. The bonds and feelings that exist between the members of a normal family offer one example. But the idea goes beyond the bounds of family. The members of a particular village or even of a given small society can be said to be characterized by Gemeinschaft. This type of relationship can develop because people are related to each other by blood, and hold each other in mutual respect; it can be produced because people are tied by tradition to a particular place where they lead a deeply integrated life; there can even be a Gemeinschaft of the mind, as where members of a religious order share a deep commitment to a given set of beliefs that become a basis for a strong social organization. The Gemeinschaft type of organization, in short, is one where people are deeply bound to each other through tradition, through kinship, through friendship, or because of some other deeply uniting factor. Such a social organization places the individual within the nexus of exceedingly strong systems of informal social control. In short, Gemeinschaft refers to a "reciprocal, binding sentiment... which keeps human beings together as members of a totality." [7] That totality may be a family, a clan, a village, a religious order, or even an entire society, but if so, it has as a basis for its common unity this particular kind of social relationship between its members.

It is clear that there probably have been few societies whose social fabric was characterized completely by such intense feeling of "community" in the sense of Gemeinschaft. However, even as an abstract construction, this "ideal type" can serve as a framework for discussing changes in social organization and new kinds of linkages between members that take place if the society evolves into some other form. For example, under the impact of industrialization, when the division of labor becomes vastly more complex through increasing specialization, is there a decline in Gemeinschaft? Tönnies saw his own homeland undergo a transition from a basically peasant society to one that was increasingly urban and industrial. While he did not suggest that societal evolution was simply a movement from Gemeinschaft in social relations to some other form, it was clear to him that another constructed polar type was going to be increasingly important to describe adequately an entirely different system of social relationships between the members of the newer society. The second of his theoretical constructs was *Gesellschaft*.

The essential condition of the social relationship in the Gesellschaft is the contract. The contract in its broadest sense is a rationally agreed upon voluntary social relationship where the two parties involved promise to fulfill specific obligations to each other or to forfeit specific commodities if the contract is breached. The contract is a formal relationship (often written, and always backed by impersonal mechanisms of social control) whereas the social relationship of the Gemeinschaft is informal. In the new society of complex credit, world markets, large formal associations, and a vast division of labor, the contractual type of relationship is widely found between members. The buyer and seller relate themselves in this way as do the employer and employee. In fact, throughout all the major social institutions, the economic order, the political structure, the educational system, religion, and even in some instances the family, the older Gemeinschaft bond, based upon "reciprocal, binding sentiment," is being replaced by relationships of the contractual type. In certain spheres of societal exchange, it is almost the exclusive kind of relationship that can exist between two parties, for example, buying or renting a dwelling. In some spheres it may seldom be found (e.g., within the family).

While no society has been or probably ever will be exclusively Gesellschaft, it is clear that this type of social bond has become ubiquitous and pervasive. It is also clear that Gesellschaft implies a very different outlook for the individual as he contemplates his fellow societal members than is the case in the Gemeinschaft.

In the Gesellschaft . . . everybody is by himself and isolated, and there exists a condition of tension against all others. Their spheres of activity are sharply separated, so that everybody refuses to everyone else contact with and admittance to his sphere; i.e., intrusions are regarded as hostile acts. Such a negative attitude toward one another becomes the normal and always underlying relation of those power-endowed individuals, and it characterizes the Gesellschaft in the condition of the rest; nobody wants to grant and produce anything for another individual, nor will he be inclined to give ungrudgingly to another individual, if it be not in exchange for a gift or labor equivalent that he considers at least equal to what he has given.[8]

The Gesellschaft, then, places the individual within a social system that is impersonal and anonymous. It is a situation where the individual is not treated or valued for himself or his personal qualities, but where he is appreciated to the degree that he can carry out his end of the contractual obligations that he assumes. The Gesellschaft is a system of competitive relationships, where each individual seeks to maximize what he gets from exchanges and minimize what he gives, and at the same time he learns to be wary of the others.

The reader will recognize that these two pictures of societal organization have been deliberately overdrawn for theoretical purposes. However, the Gemeinschaft and Gesellschaft polarity does provide a very useful framework for interpreting the impact of changing social conditions upon the citizen of the emerging industrial order. The Gemeinschaft could easily be idealized as psychologically comforting and supporting, while the Gesellschaft could easily be condemned as psychologically distressing and tension producing. Such interpretations abound in literature, in popular thought, and even in social science, where the simpler Gemeinschaft life of an earlier or more rural society is identified as "good," while the impersonal Gesellschaft of the urban area is defined as "evil." But while many have speculated in these directions, our present task is to extract from such 19th century writers as Tönnies ideas that were to influence those who turned their attentions to assessing the impact of the new media of communication on society. Just as an accumulation of theories and inventions in the natural sciences led to the physical basis upon which the media themselves were developed, the accumulation of sociological thought concerning the nature of the contemporary social order provided the basis of ideas upon which interpretations of the media were first attempted when they became realities.

Before pulling together the various concepts which we have examined into some kind of composite theoretical image of society as it was viewed by the end of the 19th century, there is one additional writer whose ideas were of particular significance. Near the end of the period (1893) Emile Durkheim published *The Division of Labor in Society*. In this important work, he brought together the several related themes which we have noted above from the writings of Comte, Spencer, and Tönnies.[9]

The overall purpose of Durkheim's extended analysis was to show how the division of labor of a society was the principal source of *social solidarity* in that society, and that as the division of labor was altered (as for example through social evolution), the unifying forces of the society underwent corresponding change. Solidarity refers to the kinds of social psychological bonds that unite the members, and although Durkheim used a very different terminology, he was addressing himself roughly toward the same general problem as Tönnies. By division of labor, Durkheim meant more than simply the degree of specialization in the economic institution:

[We must ask] if the division of labor ... in contemporary societies where it has developed as we know ... would not have as its function the integration of the social body to assure unity. It is quite legitimate to suppose ... that great political societies can maintain themselves in equilibrium only thanks to the specialization of tasks, that the division of labor is the source, if not unique, at least principal, of social solidarity. Comte took this point of view. Of all sociologists, to our knowledge, he is the first to have recognized in the division of labor something other than a purely economic phenomenon. He saw in it "the most essential condition of social life," provided that one conceives it "in all its rational extent; that is to say, that one applies it to the totality of all our diverse operations of whatever kind, instead of attributing it, as is ordinarily done, to simple material usages." [10]

To show the social implications of the division of labor, Durkheim contrasted *mechanical* and *organic* solidarity. Mechanical solidarity is that which unites a people who are essentially alike. Through their common life, and in the presence of only a rudimentary division of labor, the members of a given population work out a set of beliefs, values, and other orientations to which they are deeply, commonly, and uniformly committed. To the extent that these orientations are truly characteristic of every member, there is little basis for the development of extensive individuality. Where there is little or no division of labor, people not only act in like ways, Durkheim suggested, but think and feel in like ways. In this kind of society, "solidarity can grow only in inverse ratio to personality," because personality is what distinguishes one person from another. "If we have a strong and lively desire to think and act for ourselves, we cannot be strongly inclined to think and act as others do." [11] In the extreme case, *all* individuality would be submerged, and the members of the society would be completely *homogeneous* in their personal psychic organization. In such an admittedly theoretical case, the members of the society would be completely uniform in their action.

The social molecules which can be coherent in this way can act together only in the measure that they have no actions of their own, as the molecules of inorganic bodies. That is why we propose to call this type of solidarity mechanical. The term does not signify that it is produced by mechanical and artificial means. We call it that only by analogy to the cohesion which unites the elements of an inanimate body, as opposed to that which makes a unity out of the elements of a living body.[12]

It is perfectly obvious that no society was ever characterized completely by this kind of social organization. The idea of mechanical solidarity as a basis for binding members of a collectivity to the whole is posed in this way as an abstract construct rather than a description that is supposed to portray reality with complete accuracy. The same can be said of Durkheim's second major concept, organic solidarity. The two taken together, however, offer a third useful interpretive framework in understanding the emergence of modern society.

If mechanical solidarity is based upon *homogeneity,* then organic solidarity is based upon *heterogeneity.* In a society with a well-developed division of labor, each individual performing his specialized task is dependent upon others whose activities are coordinated with his. Spencer had elaborated in extraordinary detail the parallels between organisms and society as unified systems of reciprocally functioning parts.

Durkheim saw the mutual dependency which specialization produced, and he recognized this as a kind of social force that bound the member of society to his fellow members to form a more or less harmonious functioning whole. But the important factor is that the division of labor, which produces organic solidarity, also increases greatly the degree of individuality and *social differentiation* within the society:

Whereas the previous type [of solidarity] implies that individuals resemble each other, this type presumes their difference. The first is possible only insofar as the individual personality is absorbed into the collective personality; the second is possible only if each one has a sphere of action which is peculiar to him; that is a personality. It is necessary, then, that the collective conscience leave open a part of the individual conscience in order that special functions may be established there, functions which it cannot regulate. The more this region is extended, the stronger is the cohesion which results from this solidarity.[13]

Durkheim went on to show how the growth of the division of labor increases the dependence of each specialized person on the rest, but this does not mean that such increasing heterogeneity leads to consensus of thought. On the contrary: "Each individual is more and more acquiring his own way of thinking and acting, and submits less completely to the common corporate union." [14] Thus, while in one sense the highly specialized person is locked into a web of functional dependency upon others, he is at the same time isolated from them in a psychological sense as his specializations lead him to develop greater and greater individuality.

Durkheim also noted that the evolution of society to a more complex form leads to an increase in social relationships of much the same type that Tönnies called Gesellschaft: "It is quite true that contractual relations, which were originally rare or completely absent, multiply as social labor becomes divided." [15] Thus, an increase in the division of labor has the result not only of increasing individual heterogeneity, but of introducing an increasing number of more formal and segmental relationships between people.

Finally, Durkheim saw that under some circumstances the division of labor could result in what he called "pathological forms." "Though normally," he said, "the division of labor produces social solidarity, it sometimes happens that it has different, and even contrary results." [16] If social functions, that is parts of the organic structure, are not well articulated with each other, organic solidarity can break down. Commercial crises, depressions, strife between labor and management, civil upheavals, riots, demonstrations, and protests by subgroups offer various kinds of examples.

Thus, the very division of labor that produces harmony up to a point contains the seeds of social disharmony if pushed beyond a certain point. This, of course, was (as Durkheim noted) the thesis of Auguste Comte. Such a state of disharmony Durkheim called *anomie*. This is a kind of pathology of the social organism that results when the division of labor becomes elaborated to a point where individuals are not capable of effectively relating themselves to others.

Functional diversity induces a moral diversity that nothing can prevent, and it is inevitable that one should grow as the other does. We know, moreover, why these two phenomena develop in parallel fashion. Collective sentiments become more and more impotent in holding together the centrifugal tendencies that the division of labor is said to engender, for these tendencies increase as labor is more divided, and, at the same time, collective sentiments are weakened.[17]

In short, as society becomes more and more complex—as the members of the society become more and more preoccupied with their own individual pursuits and development—they lose ability to identify with and feel themselves in community with others. Eventually, they become a collectivity of psychologically isolated individuals, interacting with each other but oriented inward, and bound together primarily through contractual ties.

As the 19th century came to a close, this was in general the image of society that had emerged. The developing and accumulating body of sociological theory, uncoordinated and even conflicting though it was, seemed in one way or another to stress these themes. Society was a large and complex system. It was also growing much more complex. To some this represented Progress via natural laws of evolution to a more desirable and ultimately more harmonious system than before. To others, it represented an insidious movement to a bleak and isolated existence for the individual, narrowly concerned with his special pursuits, and incapable of intense identification with his fellows. Great debates arose concerning the advisability of interfering with the evolution of society through legislation. Other arguments arose concerning the best possible strategy for proceeding with the further development of theories about these vast changes. But in spite of these divergent points of view over strategies and consequences, it seemed clear to most students of the social order that the Western world was experiencing an increase in heterogeneity and individuality, a reduction in the degree to which society could effectively control its members through informal means, an increasing alienation of the individual from strong identification with his community as a whole, a growth of segmental, contractual social relationships, and a great increase in the psychological isolation of the human being.

These general social trends were said to be leading to the *mass society*. The idea of mass society is not equivalent to *massive society,* that is, to large numbers. There are many societies in the world, for example, India, that have astronomical numbers of people, but are still more or less traditional in their organization. Mass society refers to the relationship that exists between an individual member and the social order around him. In mass society, as has been emphasized in the theories we have examined, the individual is presumed to be in a situation of psychological isolation from others, impersonality is said to prevail in his interactions with others, and he is said to be relatively free from the demands of binding social obligations. These ideas have been carried by some sociologists well into the 20th century, and are still important considerations, along with a number of modifications and countertrends.[18] In discussing the organization of the urban industrial social order of the contemporary Western world, Broom and Selznick have recently summarized the principal outlines of the idea of mass society very succinctly in the following terms:

Modern society is made up of masses in the sense that "there has emerged a vast mass of segregated, isolated individuals, interdependent in all sorts of specialized ways yet lacking in any central unifying value or purpose." The weakening of traditional bonds, the growth of rationality, and the division of labor, have created societies made up of individuals who are only loosely bound together. In this sense the word "mass" suggests something closer to an aggregate than to a tightly knit social group.[19]

This view of the *social* nature of man was coupled with an equally developed general theory of his *psychological* nature. Briefly, man's conduct was thought to be largely a product of his genetic endowment. That is, the causes of behavior were sought within his biological structure. This line of thought was to have important implications for the early interpretation of the new mass media. The nature of general psychological theory and its importance in interpreting the mass media will be made clear in later sections.

WORLD WAR I AND THE MECHANISTIC S-R THEORY

It was against this intellectual backdrop that the mass media of communication diffused through the major Western societies during their early years. To assess the influence that such general theories of the nature of man had upon some of the early thinking about the media, we need to look briefly to the period when mass communication was still a relatively new social phenomenon with which the world had to contend.

The first decade of the 20th century had barely passed before Europe and later the United States were plunged into the Great War. The very division of labor and the resulting heterogeneity and individuality that had made the new industrial societies possible now became a problem. World War I was really the first of the global struggles in which entire populations played active and coordinated roles in the effort against their enemies. In most previous wars, the opposing military forces carried on their struggles somewhat independently of civilian populations. Unless combat happened to take place in their immediate area, the people left at home were not deeply and personally involved. This had been particularly true of England, which had not been occupied by an enemy since the Norman invasion. It was also true of the United States, which had last known foreign soldiers on its shores during Revolutionary times, although the Civil War had brought great hardships in some areas.

But the new kind of war was, in effect, a pitting of the manufacturing capacity of one nation against that of the other, and the armies in the field were backed by and totally dependent upon vast industrial complexes at home. These huge industrial efforts required the whole-hearted cooperation and enthusiasm of the civilian populations who manned them. Total war required total commitment of the entire resources of the nation. Material amenities had to be sacrificed; morale had to be maintained; young men had to be persuaded away from their families and into the ranks; the work in the factories had to be done with unflagging vigor; and not the least important, money had to be obtained to finance the war.

But the diverse, heterogeneous, and differentiated populations of the industrial societies were not bound together by that "reciprocal, binding sentiment ... which keeps human beings together as members of a totality." [20] They were not Gemeinschaft societies, but were in fact more like mass societies, which lacked such effective bonds. Yet, it was just such bonds of sentiment that were needed to unite these people into effective solidarity behind their respective war efforts. As each country became politically committed to the war, there arose a most critical and urgent need to forge stronger links between the individual and his society. It became *essential* to mobilize his sentiments and loyalties, to instill in him a hatred and fear of the enemy, to maintain his morale in the face of privation, and to capture his energies into an effective contribution to his nation.

The means for achieving these urgent goals was *propaganda*. Carefully designed propaganda messages engulfed the nation in news stories, pictures, films, phonograph records, speeches, books, sermons, posters, wireless signals, rumors, billboard advertisements, and handbills. Top level policy makers decided the stakes were so high and the ends were so important, that they justified almost any means. The citizen had to hate the enemy, love his country, and maximize his commitment to the war effort. He could not be depended upon to do so on his own. The mass media of communication available at the time became the principal tools for persuading him to do so.

Following the war, a number of persons who had been importantly involved in the manufacturing of propaganda were ridden with guilt about the gross deceptions which they had practiced. Outrageous lies were told by one side about the other, and when placed before the populations of the time via the mass media, they were often believed. Such large scale persuasion of entire populations with the use of mass media had never been seen before, and it was conducted in a skillful and highly coordinated manner. Also, those were apparently more innocent times; even the word "propaganda" was not understood by the man in the street. After the war, when former propagandists published a rash of sensational exposés about their wartime deceptions, the general public became more sophisticated.

But to illustrate briefly the kinds of material the propagandists found effective and the kinds of responses to their stimuli that they were seeking, the following is quoted from one widely read postwar exposé:

The Atrocity Story was one big factor in English propaganda. Most ... were greedily swallowed by an unsuspecting public. They would have been less ready to accept the stories of German frightfulness if they had witnessed the birth of the most lugubrious atrocity story at the headquarters of the British Intelligence Department in the Spring of 1917.

Brigadier General J.V. Charteris...was comparing two pictures captured from the Germans. The first was a vivid reproduction of a harrowing scene, showing the dead bodies of German soldiers being hauled away for burial behind the lines. The second picture depicted dead horses on their way to the factory where German ingenuity extracted soap and oil from the carcasses. The inspiration to change the captions of the two pictures came to General Charteris like a flash.

...the General dexterously used the shears and pasted the inscription "German Cadavers on Their Way to the Soap Factory" under the dead German soldiers. Within twenty-four hours the picture was in the mail-pouch for Shanghai.

General Charteris dispatched the picture to China to revolt public opinion against the Germans. The reverence of the Chinese for the dead amounts to worship. The profanation of the dead ascribed to the Germans was one of the factors responsible for the Chinese declaration of war against the central powers.[21]

Whether this particular propagandist was correct in his assessment of the impact of this falsified newspaper picture need not concern us. The example and the claimed effect give a classic illustration of the kind of theory of mass communication upon which such propaganda efforts were premised. It was a relatively simple theory and it was consistent with the image of mass society that was the intellectual heritage from the 19th century. It assumed that cleverly designed stimuli would reach every individual member of the mass society via the media, that each would perceive it in the same general manner as his fellows, and that this would provoke a more or less uniform response from all.

In the aftermath of the war, there emerged a quite general belief in the great power of mass communication. The media were thought to be able to shape public opinion and to sway the masses toward almost any point of view desired by the communicator. An American political scientist who tried to analyze objectively the impact of wartime propaganda and the role of the media in the mass society came to these conclusions:

But when all allowances have been made, and all extravagant estimates pared to the bone, the fact remains that propaganda is one of the most powerful instrumentalities in the modern world. It has arisen to its present eminence in response to a complex of changed circumstances which have altered the nature of society. Small primitive tribes can weld their heterogeneous members into a fighting whole by the beat of the tom-tom and the tempestuous rhythm of the dance. It is in orgies of physical exuberance that young men are brought to the boiling point of war, and that old and young, men and women, are caught in the suction of tribal purpose.

In the Great Society it is no longer possible to fuse the waywardness of individuals in the furnace of the war dance; a newer and subtler instrument must weld thousands and even millions of human beings into one amalgamated mass of hate and will and hope. A new flame must burn out the canker of dissent and temper the steel of bellicose enthusiasm. The name of this new hammer and anvil of social solidarity is propaganda.[22]

The basic theory of mass communication that is implied by such conclusions is not quite as simple as it might appear. To be sure, it is relatively straightforward S-R theory, but it is also one that presumes a particular set of unspoken assumptions concerning not only the social organization of society, but the psychological structure of the human beings who are being stimulated and who are responding to the mass communicated message. It is important to understand the full range of these implicit assumptions because *it has been through their systematic replacement or modification* that more modern theories of the mass communication process have been developed. As new concepts concerning the nature of man as an individual and the nature of his society became available, these were used to modify the basic theory of mass communication by introducing different sets of intervening variables between the stimulus side of the S-R equation and the response side.

We may refer to the first mass communication theory as a "mechanistic S-R theory." It has been given other more colorful names such as "hypodermic needle theory," "transmission belt theory," etc., but these seem to overlook its more basic underlying assumptions. While it may appear to be unrealistic in view of today's more adequate perspectives, it is not true that it was simply a *direct* S-R theory. There was more to its structure than what such writers as Katz and Lazarsfeld have suggested, namely, ". . . the omnipotent media, on the one hand, sending forth the message, and the atomized masses, on the other, waiting to receive it—*and nothing in between* [italics added]." [23] There were very definite assumptions about what was going on in between. These assumptions may not have been explicitly formulated at the time, but they were drawn from fairly elaborate theories of human nature, as well as the nature of the social order (which we have already examined). It was these theories that guided the thinking of those who saw the media as powerful.

World War I was a period when *instinct* psychology was at its peak.

It was not until the end of the 1920's that the facts of human individual modifiability and variability began to be demonstrable with the use of new mental tests and other research techniques. As a consequence, the image of man represented by the writings of William MacDougal and his contemporaries was called into serious question. Prior to that time, it was assumed that a given individual's behavior was governed to a considerable extent by inherited biological mechanisms of some complexity that intervened between the stimuli and his responses. Because of this, basic human nature was thought to be fairly *uniform* from one human being to another. Each person inherited (according to the theories) more or less the same elaborate set of built-in biological mechanisms, which supplied him with motivations and energies to respond to given stimuli in given ways. Much was made of the non-rational or emotional nature of such mechanisms, particularly among theorists of psychoanalytic bent. But even these were, in the final analysis, inherited forces (e.g., libido), which each person received at birth in more or less uniform degrees. The psychology of individual differences had not progressed to the point where a consuming interest in learning would develop among academic psychologists as a means of accounting for such differences.

Given a view of a uniform basic human nature, with a stress upon nonrational processes, plus a view of the social order as mass society, the mechanistic S-R theory of the media as powerful devices seemed entirely valid: It stated that powerful stimuli were uniformly brought to the attention of the individual members of the mass. These stimuli tapped inner urges, emotions, or other processes over which the individual had little voluntary control. Because of the inherited nature of these mechanisms, each person responded more or less uniformly. Furthermore, there were few strong social ties to disrupt the influence of these mechanisms because he was psychologically isolated from strong social ties and informal social control. The result was that the members of the mass could be swayed and influenced by those in possession of the media especially with the use of emotional appeals.

Such a mechanistic theory was completely consistent with general theory in both sociology and psychology as it had been developed up to that time. In addition, there was the example of the tremendous impact of wartime propaganda. This *seemed* to offer valid proof that the media *were* powerful in precisely the manner so dramatically described by Lasswell when he concluded that they were the "new hammer and anvil of social solidarity." [24] There were also the seemingly undisputable facts from the mass advertising of the time that the media were capable of persuading people to buy goods in degrees and variety hitherto undreamed of. This added to the conviction of great power and it reinforced the seeming validity of the mechanistic S-R theory.[25]

There is no doubt that World War I propaganda was effective. However, this does not mean that only one theory is capable of accounting for those effects. If scholars of the day had been in possession of the results of research and thought on mass communication which have accumulated since that time, they might have chosen very different explanations indeed to account for the fact that the population of the United States entered the war with enthusiasm, entertained a series of unrealistic beliefs about the enemy, etc., and that the media played a part in shaping their behavior and beliefs.

But theories of man, both in terms of his social order and his personal organization, did not remain static. In the United States, both psychology and sociology had become more firmly established and were increasingly escaping the domination of the thoughtways of their European origins. Both fields became heavily concerned with empirical research. As a result, their theories were forced to be more closely checked against reality. In consequence, many earlier ideas were abandoned and many new ideas were advanced. Inevitably, these new theoretical directions had their impact on those who were attempting to understand the effects of mass communication. The mechanistic S-R theory had been built upon assumptions that were no longer regarded as tenable by general theorists, and consequently the theory had to be rather reluctantly abandoned by students of the mass media. In the meantime, there was very little to take its place. However, even as newer general theories were being devised to describe man's nature and the nature of his social order more adequately, the field of mass communication itself was acquiring an *empirical* base. During the 1930's scholars developed an interest in the media as objects of research, and were beginning to turn away from mere speculation about their effects to systematic studies of the impact of particular communication content upon particular kinds of people. As an increasing variety of research tools became available to them, their ideas about mass communication could be more adequately checked against their findings. Thus, the field of mass communication began to accumulate a body of data from which concepts and propositions could be inductively formulated. Even so, the field continued to be greatly influenced by trends in more general behavioral science, as the following chapter will attempt to show.

Chapter VII

CONTEMPORARY THEORIES
OF MASS COMMUNICATION

THE ALL-CONSUMING question that has dominated research and the development of contemporary theory in the study of the mass media can be summed up in simple terms—namely, "what has been their effect?" That is, how have the media influenced us as individuals in terms of persuading us to believe in new political ideologies, to vote for a particular party, to purchase more goods, to alter or abandon our cultural tastes, to reduce or strengthen our prejudices, to commit acts of delinquency or crime, to lower our standards of sexual morality, to alter our patterns of family recreation, to adopt an innovation, or to change our patterns of behavior in some other significant way as a result of attention to the content of mass communication? If from time to time attention has been given to some other aspect of the media, for example, to the nature of the communicator, the structure of media content, or the nature of audiences, the ultimate purpose was to see how variations in these factors have influenced the kinds of responses that have resulted from exposure to the media.[1] In a recent overview of research in the field, Larsen has stated the issue in the following terms:

> All over the world more and more people are spending more and more time in exposure to the media of mass communication. The present task is to inquire into how sociologists have come to grips with the social consequences of this fact. The goal is to review what has been done and to suggest what might be done to understand the social effects of mass communication.[2]

For several decades, sociologists and other social scientists have attempted to "come to grips with this fact" by seeking theoretical frameworks aimed at ordering in some systematic way a tremendous diversity of observations about the effects of mass communication and the variables that modify them. As was suggested in the previous chapter, the formulations offered to date have been more or less consistent with trends in general behavioral science theory. The goal of the present chapter is to indicate in overview how theoretical propositions concerning mass communication have become increasingly elaborated as interest in the field has grown and as developments in more general theory and research have made available an increasing variety of conceptual tools and techniques of investigation.

At the same time, the overwhelming concentration on *effect*, which has characterized mass communication as an object of research, cannot be passed over lightly. There are other theoretical and research questions of significance that can be asked about the media. This was indicated in detail in earlier chapters where attention was focused upon the nature of the communication process and some of the ways in which the media themselves were influenced by the nature of the society within which they developed. Until adequate formulations have been advanced concerning the impact of societies with given characteristics on their developing media, and upon the manner in which media operate within particular societal systems, theories of mass communication will be hopelessly one-sided.[3]

But meanwhile, thinking concerning the impact of the media on individuals and groups has undergone progressive change. This change has for the most part been a continuous and cumulative discovery of important intervening processes between media and mass, that is between the stimulus and the response sides of the S-R equation. There has also been an increasing development of more elaborate classifications of different types of mass communication stimuli and different types of responses that the media can evoke. These assertions can be elaborated in the form of four specific formulations that summarize contemporary thinking about the effects of mass communications.

THE INDIVIDUAL DIFFERENCES THEORY

When psychological theorists seeking basic understanding of human conduct turned away from explanations of complex behavior based primarily upon inherited mechanisms, they sought new explanations built upon very different principles. If nature failed to endow the human individual with the automatic ability to guide his behavior, then he surely had to *acquire* it from the environment around him. Great interest was to develop among psychologists in the process of human learning. By the end of World War I, academic psychology was intellectually prepared for new directions. One new direction was provided by the concept of *conditioning*.

From English empiricism, psychologists had inherited a persistent interest in "association" and "habit" as important aspects of learning. Laws of association had been repeatedly formulated and even as early as 1890 William James had suggested that habits that were formed through association might have a physiological basis.[4] John Watson introduced a further significant element to modern psychology with his objective emphasis on *behaviorism*.[5] But more than anything else, it was the classical conditioning experiments that fired the imagination of the psychologists of the late 1920's and the early 1930's.[6] Thus, there was a renewed interest in habit formation through learning, a new stress upon objective experiments as an aid in the development of theories of learning, and a broad new concept that promised to link the learning process to physiology. The result of these intellectual trends was a great expansion of interest in the learning process and a host of experiments with animals and human subjects. A number of competing theories of learning were formulated.

Along with this intellectual movement came an associated interest in such processes as "motivation." The study of incentives in laboratory experiments convinced psychologists that some motivational urges can be acquired through learning and that not all individuals can be motivated by precisely the same incentives. Adding to this trend in the increasing recognition of individual motivation and learning *differences* were the findings of students of human personality. Variations among individuals in their personality traits became increasingly recognized, and the mental testers began to construct sophisticated devices to quantify those differences.[7]

New concepts were also formulated in social psychology to replace the idea of instinct. In particular, the term "attitude" grew in importance as a means of explaining differing directions of human preference and action. Introduced as a systematic concept in the writings of Thomas and Znaniecki, at the end of World War I, this concept became the most basic and central theoretical tool of social psychology.[8] The invention of several rather elaborate and mathematically sophisticated techniques for attitude measurement added to its importance as a research tool and gave additional emphasis to the study of individual differences and their correlates.[9]

As these basic ideas concerning the psychological organization of the human individual were successively clarified, certain fundamental postulates became rather widely held. In brief summary, these were more or less as follows: First, human beings *varied* greatly in their personal psychological organization. These variations in part began with differential biological endowment, but they were due in greater measure to differential learning. Human beings raised under widely differing circumstances were exposed to widely differing points of view. From these learning environments they acquired a set of attitudes, values, and beliefs that constituted their personal psychological make-up and set each somewhat apart from his fellows. Even twins of almost identical biological make-up became rather different in personality structure when raised in different social environments.

Added to this increasing recognition of human psychological modifiability and differentiation was the recognition that personality variables acquired from the social milieu provided a basis for viewing or *perceiving* particular events from quite different perspectives from one person to another. The experimental study of human perception had revealed that the individual's values, needs, beliefs, and attitudes played an influential role in determining how he selected stimuli from the environment and the way he attributed meaning to those stimuli within his acquired frames of reference once they came to his attention. Thus, one important product of human learning was the acquisition of stable predispositions or habits concerning the perception of events around him. Perception differed systematically from one person to another according to the nature of his personality structure.

With these new theories in the background, students of mass communication had to alter their thinking about the media. It became clear that the audience of a given medium was not a monolithic collectivity whose members attended uniformly to whatever content was directed toward them. The *principle of selective attention and perception* was formulated as a fundamental proposition regarding the communication behavior of the ordinary person. General psychological theory had established the concept of selective perception based upon individual differences in personality characteristics. It was not difficult to show that different types of people in an audience selected and interpreted mass communication content in widely varying ways.[10]

Although never specifically formulated as a theory, it can be suggested that selective attention and perception had become intervening psychological mechanisms that were entered into the S-R schema of mass communication theory in an attempt to explain differential response. From a multiplicity of available content, the member of the audience selectively attended to messages, particularly if they were related to his interests, consistent with his attitudes, congruent with his beliefs, and supportive of his values. His response to such messages was modified by his psychological make-up. At the risk of attributing to it a more systematic nature than it may in fact have had, this general idea may be called the *individual differences theory of mass communication effects*. Rather than being *uniform* among the mass audience, the effects of the media could now be seen as *varying* from person to person because of individual differences in psychological structure.

When communication "effects" are a focus of research attention, the assumption that the media are in some way "causes" of those effects is a natural one. Even if it is granted that intervening processes of some sort can soften or otherwise modify this relationship, the underlying cause-effect conceptualization is not different, only more complicated. The individual differences theory of mass communication implies that media messages contain particular stimulus attributes that have differential interaction with personality characteristics of members of the audience. Since there are individual differences in personality characteristics among such members, it is natural to assume that there will be variations in effect which correspond to such individual differences. However, by holding constant the mediating influence of personality variables (that is by considering people with similar personality characteristics), such a theory would still predict uniformity of response to a given message (if the intervening variables operate uniformly). Thus, the logical structure of the individual differences theory is a "cause-(intervening processes)-effect" structure, just as was the mechanistic S-R theory before it. However, the intervening processes are the result of learning rather than inheritance.

The Social Categories Theory

Sometimes overlapping the individual differences theory, but stemming from completely different disciplinary sources, is the *social categories theory*. The latter assumes that there are broad collectivities, aggregates, or social categories in urban-industrial societies whose behavior in the face of a given set of stimuli is more or less uniform. Such characteristics as age, sex, income level, educational attainment, rural-urban residence, or religious affiliation provide examples. Simple illustrations concerning mass communication are the facts that fashion magazines are not often bought by males; fishing magazines are seldom read by females. In fact, knowledge of several very simple variables—age, sex, and educational attainment—provides a reasonably accurate guide to the type of communication content a given individual will or will not select from available media. A highly educated older male would probably never read "true confession" type magazines, while a poorly educated young woman probably would with some frequency.

An early research trend in mass media studies made such category membership a central focus. It sought to establish the ways in which such behaviors as newspaper reading, the selection of books, radio listening, and motion picture attendance were related to a variety of simple characteristics by which people could be grouped into aggregates.[11]

The basic assumption of the social categories theory is a sociological one—namely, that in spite of the heterogeneity of modern society, people who have a number of similar characteristics will have similar folkways. These similar modes of orientation and behavior will relate them to such phenomena as the mass media in a fairly uniform manner. The members of a particular category will select more or less the same communication content and will respond to it in roughly equal ways. The social categories theory is less an explanatory formulation than a kind of descriptive formula, but insofar as it can serve as a basis for rough prediction and as a guide for research, it has functioned as a simplistic theory in the study of the mass media.

Actually, it has a more complex theoretical basis than is apparent on the surface. It will be recalled that the sociological theorists of the 19th century stressed the increasing degree of social differentiation that was taking place in the developing industrial society. In the society with a rudimentary division of labor, Durkheim had suggested, people would be very much alike. But in a society with a complex division of labor, there would be much greater development of personality. However, most such theorists had stressed the idea that people located at similar positions in this social structure would be attracted to each other and form categories that were somewhat homogeneous. Comte had suggested that these people who formed groupings on the basis of similar characteristics would become a "multitude of unconnected corporations, which almost seem not to belong to the same species" [12] (i.e., subcultures).

While the individual differences theory presented a view of the communication process more consistent with findings in general psychology, the social categories theory was consistent with and seemingly derived from general sociological theories of the nature of the mass society. Taken together, they brought contemporary mass communication theory to a point where both the social differentiation of the early sociological theorists, and the individual differences of the personality theorists were taken into account. Both of these theories represent modifications of the original mechanistic S-R theory, substituting on the one hand latent psychological processes and on the other uniformities within social categories as intervening variables between communication stimuli and responses. Both take into account the idea that variations in stimulus factors, in media, in content, as well as in audience, can have a far-reaching influence on the effects achieved by mass communication. In fact, in 1948 Lasswell summed up precisely these two theories and the situational variables related to them, when he stated that "A convenient way to describe an act of communication is to answer the following questions: [13]

> Who
> Says What
> In Which Channel
> To Whom
> With What Effect?

While these two theories of mass communication remain useful and contemporary, there have been further additions to the set of variables intervening between media stimuli and audience response. This additional elaboration of the S-R formula represents a somewhat belated recognition of the role of patterns of interaction *between* audience members.

THE SOCIAL RELATIONSHIPS THEORY

Like many other significant discoveries in science, the role of group relationships in the mass communication process seems to have been discovered almost by accident. Also, like many other important ideas, it appears to have been independently discovered at about the same time by more than one researcher working independently. From the standpoint of mass communication research on "effects," one study stands out as the context within which the important role of group ties, as a complex of intervening variables between media and audience influence, was recognized forcefully. Early in 1940, Lazarsfeld, Berelson, and Gaudet developed an elaborate research design to study the impact upon voters of that year's mass communicated Presidential election campaign. At first, they were interested in how the members of given social categories selected material related to the election from the media, and how this material played a part in influencing their voting intentions.[14]

Erie County, Ohio, a rather typical American area, had voted as the nation voted in every prior Presidential election, and this county was chosen as a site for the research. The mass communications of the Presidential election campaign of Wendell Willkie vs. Franklin D. Roosevelt constituted the stimulus material, and several representative samples of residents of the area were the subjects. The study used an imaginative procedure that permitted repeated interviewing of a 600-member panel with suitable controls to check for possible effects of the seven independent monthly visits of the interviewers. The effects under study were several. Participation in the campaign, that is, paying attention to it and seeking out information about the candidates and the issues, was one effect. Formulating a decision for whom to vote was another. Finally, of course, actually going to the polls to vote was still another. As it turned out, there were still other kinds of effects that could be attributed to the campaign. Some respondents were *activated* by the mass communicated material. That is, they had latent predispositions to vote in a given direction, but these predispositions needed to be crystallized to the point where they would become manifest. Others among the electorate had pretty much made up their minds early in the campaign, and these decisions were *reinforced* by a continuous and partisan selection of additional material from the media. Finally, for only a handful, early vote intentions were reversed, and the campaign succeeded in *converting* the individual from one party to another.

The influence of the social categories theory as a guide to this research was clear:

. . . The most interested people were better-educated, better-off, older, urban men. These same characteristics are associated with high exposure to political communications. There are good cultural reasons to explain this. The better educated have more intellectual equipment and more civic training. The better-off have a greater awareness about politics and think they have a larger stake in it. The older also think they have a bigger stake in politics; in addition, the younger people in this country, unlike the youth of Europe, are not particularly politically conscious. The urban find it easier to expose to communications, especially print, because there are more opportunities to do so in the city than in the country. And finally, men are compelled by the mores to pay attention to politics and women are not.[15]

Age, sex, residence, economic status, and education were the key variables. These social category memberships determined "interest" and led to an early or late decision. Acting in concert, this complex of variables influenced the individual's degree and direction of exposure to the mass communicated campaign material, on the one hand, and the kinds of effects that such material would have upon him, on the other hand.

As has been suggested, designing the study around this kind of search for the important intervening social categories was perfectly consistent with the mass society concepts that communication researchers had inherited from European sociological theorists. Little attention was given to the possible role of informal social relationships and such factors as primary group ties, because these were presumed to be declining in the emerging *Gesellschaft* society. Elihu Katz has stated this argument cogently in the following terms:

Until very recently, the image of society in the minds of most students of communication was of atomized individuals, connected with the mass media, but not with one another. Society—the "audience"—was conceived of as aggregates of age, sex, social class, and the like, but little thought was given to the relationships implied thereby to more informal relationships. The point is not that the student of mass communication was unaware that members of the audience have families and friends but that he did not believe that they might affect the outcome of a campaign; informal interpersonal relations, thus, were considered irrelevant to the institutions of modern society.[16]

But when the interviewers talked with the people of Erie County, they kept getting somewhat unanticipated answers to one of their major lines of questioning. "Whenever the respondents were asked to report on their recent exposures to campaign communications of all kinds, *political discussions* [italics added] were mentioned more frequently than exposure to radio or print." [17] As a matter of fact, on an average day during the election campaign period, about 10 percent more people engaged in some sort of informal exchange of ideas with *other persons* than were exposed to campaign material directly from the mass media. About midway through the series of interviews, the researchers began to probe systematically into this kind of personal influence in an attempt to unravel the role of informal contacts with other people as an important set of variables in determining the effects of the media.

The end result of this somewhat unanticipated turn of events was the recognition that *informal social relationships* play a significant role in modifying the manner in which a given individual will act upon a message which comes to his attention via the mass media. In fact, it was discovered that there were many persons whose firsthand exposure to the media was quite limited. In large part, such people obtained their information about the election campaign from other people who *had* gotten it firsthand. Thus, the research began to suggest that there was a kind of movement of information through two basic stages. First, information moved from the media to relatively well-informed individuals who attended to mass communications firsthand. Second, it moved from those persons through interpersonal channels to individuals who had less direct exposure to the media and who depended upon others for their information. This kind of communication process was termed the "two-step flow of communication." [18]

Those individuals who were more in contact with the media were called "opinion leaders," because it was soon discovered that they were playing an important role in helping to shape the vote intentions of those to whom they were passing on information. They were not only passing on information, of course, but they were passing on their *interpretations* of the communication content they had been exposed to. This kind of "personal influence" became immediately recognized as an important intervening mechanism, which operated between the mass communication message (campaign) and the kind of responses (voting behavior) made to that message.

Subsequent studies were aimed more directly at studying the mechanisms of interpersonal influence, and the part played by social relationships in mediating the movement of information from the media to the masses. In fact, a rich literature has accumulated indicating that informal social relationships operate as important intervening variables between the stimulus and the response in the mass communication process.

It was suggested earlier that the role of informal social relationships in the communication process was independently discovered by more than one researcher at about the same time. Students of rural sociology had long recognized that a farmer's informal social relationships played an important part in determining his propensity to adopt a given agricultural innovation. The rural society is one where the individual farm family normally has strong social ties with its neighbors. When new ideas come from the outside, the interpretations made by neighbors in such a setting can be of critical importance in determining the likelihood of adoption. The adoption of new farm technology is a process closely related to the mass communication process. New ideas are first presented to farm operators via communication media of one kind or another. These may be mass communication media, or they may be other formal channels of communication such as county agents, agricultural experiment station bulletins, or others. The question is whether or not the individual farmer will respond to such communications in ways advocated by the communicator, namely by adopting the recommended practice. Thus, conceptually speaking, there is a considerable similarity between the case of a farmer being advised to adopt a new form of weed spray via a radio program devoted to farm problems and the case of a housewife being advised to adopt a new household detergent via a radio commercial designed to sell soap. Both can adopt the innovation in accordance with the communicated suggestion or they can resist it. The mechanisms that operate to mediate the decision to adopt or not to adopt may be quite similar in each case.[19]

The recognition of the convergence of theory between the students of mass communication and students of rural sociology who were studying the diffusion of farm technology stimulated a surge of interest in the diffusion and adoption process insofar as it was linked to mass communication. Intensive studies were undertaken concerning the nature of opinion leadership, the way it functioned in various contexts, and the part played by interpersonal relationships. In general it has been found that opinion leaders who are influential in the adoption process are in some respects very much like those whom they influence. They tend to conform closely to the norms of their groups and they tend to be leaders in one area but not necessarily in others.[20] Opinion leadership does not seem to travel down the social structure, but is more likely to be horizontal. It appears to take place primarily between persons of somewhat similar status, although this is not always true. In some respects opinion leaders differ from their followers, but this can be complicated by the type of object or issue with respect to which they are exerting their leadership. Katz and Lazarsfeld found that position in the "life cycle" was a key variable in determining who would influence whom in areas such as marketing, fashions, and public issues.[21] Young working girls, in closer contact with fashion magazines and other media of information about such issues, were sought by the less informed for advice about hair styles, clothing, etc. Matrons with larger families, who were well informed from appropriate media sources about household products, were sought as advisers on marketing, trying out new products, etc. Thus, a woman's age, marital status, and number of children predisposed her to acquire information about issues related to her roles. These in turn were the criteria used by those needing advice on particular subjects when they turned to an opinion leader for information and influence.

The exact conditions under which a given person emerges as an opinion leader need further study. Also, the conditions that lead to his institutionalization—his relatively permanent establishment—as an opinion leader also need additional research. De Fleur has suggested a number of conditions of social structure and of social functioning that will lead to the emergence and functioning of an opinion leader.[22] A number of hypotheses concerning this issue have been studied in imaginative experimental small-groups studies by El-Assal.[23] Such experiments may eventually lead to rigorous theories of opinion leadership.

THE CULTURAL NORMS THEORY

A fourth and more controversial set of hypotheses concerning the way in which mass communications may influence behavior can be called the *cultural norms theory*. While this idea has received little in the way of explicit formulation in the communications research literature, it has been implicit in thinking and writing about the media for a long time. It appears to be the basis for much criticism of the media for their purported "harmful" effects. Essentially, the cultural norms theory postulates that the mass media, through selective presentations and the emphasis of certain themes, create impressions among their audiences that common cultural norms concerning the emphasized topics are structured or defined in some specific way. Since individual behavior is usually guided by cultural norms (or the actor's impressions of what the norms are) with respect to a given topic or situation, the media would then serve *indirectly* to influence conduct. Stated in social psychological terms, the media are said to provide a "definition of the situation" which the actor believes to be real. This definition provides guides for action which appear to be approved and supported by society. Therefore, conduct is indirectly shaped by exposure to communications.

There are at least three ways in which the media can (potentially) influence norms and definitions of the situation for individuals. First, mass communication content can *reinforce existing patterns* and lead people to believe that given social forms are being maintained by the society. Second, the media can *create new shared convictions* with respect to topics with which the public has had little prior experience. Third, they can *change existing norms* and thereby convert people from one form of behavior to another.

But do the media actually do these things? What are the ways in which mass communication content has been shown to influence social and cultural norms—thereby altering people's behavior with respect to the objects of those norms? Also, what are some of the factors and situations which either facilitate or inhibit the achievement of such effects? As will be seen, the answers to these questions are by no means simple. Furthermore, relevant research addressed specifically to these issues has as yet provided few trustworthy answers.

Concerning the first potential media-norm relationship, an older but frequently cited essay by Lazarsfeld and Merton made much of the reinforcing function of the media.[24] These authors maintained that the media operate conservatively and *follow* public norms in such matters as tastes and values, rather than lead them to new forms. Thus, they said that the media reinforce the *status quo* rather than create new norms of significance or change deeply institutionalized patterns. This view has obvious merit, at least in part. It can be granted that certain of the media appear to be at the forefront of some kinds of changes (e.g., fashion magazines). It can also be granted that there are media which sometimes transgress conservative standards by emphasizing controversial themes (e.g., movies with frank sex portrayals). By and large, however, the media do appear to be quite conservative. Television programs, for example, have not yet openly advocated religious blasphemy, free love, political anarchy, or a de-emphasis on education. No major medium has come out strongly for dropping English in favor of Esperanto or some other language. Thus, while the media continuously attempt to influence us to change in essentially trivial matters—to buy new products, wear new clothing styles, or dance in different ways—they generally avoid posing serious challenges to fundamental values or deeply established ways of doing things in our society.

At the same time, the media sometimes stimulate new forms of behavior that receive widespread social approval. Under certain circumstances, in other words, they create new cultural norms. In earlier chapters we have indicated how widespread habits such as newspaper-reading, movie-attendance, and radio-listening were quickly established when the media became available. The appearance of the TV brought new norms concerning mass communication behavior. The media collectively brought many new forms of recreation and even family interaction. There have also been other innovations in normative behavior which have been brought about by the media. Numerous illustrations could be cited. When sound movies were relatively new, for example, a favorite weekly serial featured Tarzan and assorted jungle companions. Boys of every neighborhood became proficient in thumping their chests and emitting loud shrieks in the manner of the fictional hero who behaved similarly while swinging from vine to vine. In the 1950's, after TV had been widely adopted, no red-blooded youngster in our society would have been caught without a "Davy Crockett" hat. This furry garment probably set the raccoon population of the United States back fifty years when a television program featuring a version of an historical figure made such hats enormously popular. Many readers will recall the now venerable "hula hoop," which America's chiropractors no doubt remember warmly. That incredible fad was also touched off by TV. Then there was the period of the "mouse-keteers." Perhaps the less said about *that* the better; children in all walks of life insisted upon appearing in public wearing a ridiculous black cap supporting two very large and protruding mouse ears. In any case, these widely adopted behaviors are examples of (rather transitory) norms created almost wholly by the media. Other norms of a less transitory nature, and more relevant to adults, would not be difficult to identify (e.g., widespread viewing of televised professional football and baseball games on weekends during certain seasons of the year). Thus, in some instances at least, the media can create new norms.

The issue of whether or not the media can convert people from one established form of behavior to another through altering their definition of the situation remains a thorny one. One school of thought on the matter denies that the media have much power to convert in well-established behavioral areas.[25] However, the research mind should not yet be closed on this issue. For example, current media campaigns sponsored by such groups as the American Cancer Society are intended to discourage the public from smoking cigarettes—to convert them from smoking to abstinence. There is one unmistakable sign that deeply established norms concerning this widespread habit are beginning to change slightly. For the first time in history, fewer cigarettes were smoked by the American population in a given year (1968) than in the previous year. While this is far from conversion, one can speculate that given a long time, intensive media campaigns might make substantial inroads on the normative system that underlies smoking behavior. Complicating the interpretation, of course, is the fact that smoking has some aspects of addiction—which can make elimination of the habit quite difficult. On the other hand, its medical threat would appear to make the task of persuasion easier.

Also complicating efforts to unravel the role of the media as such in this issue is the fact that mass communications are by no means the only efforts directed toward achieving this change. Various groups, including the medical profession and even Congress, have undertaken to discourage the habit. Furthermore, the efforts of individuals attempting to dissuade their friends and relatives may be a potent factor. Meanwhile, the vast majority of those who smoked prior to the campaigns still do so, and unknown numbers of new smokers have been added to the ranks of tobacco consumers, replacing those who have presumably expired from the effects of their habit. Thus, a concerted effort on the part of the media to convert a population away from an irrational, expensive, and unhealthy habit has actually had very little real success.

Another phenomenon that provides observations on the potential conversion power of the media is *prejudice*. At one time the media continuously reinforced the culture of prejudice by stereotyped portrayals of racial and ethnic types and by specific emphases on content. For example, in earlier years it was common for the media to portray members of certain minority groups in very unflattering terms. Research on magazine fiction during the 1940's showed clearly that minority members were portrayed relatively unsympathetically while members of the dominant segment of our society were treated much more favorably.[26] During the 1930's and 1940's, the movies routinely portrayed black people in humble or even degrading roles. They were cast as servants, field hands, shoe-shine boys, or even convicts. If a black person did obtain a leading part, it was almost always as some sort of clownlike character—often with an amusing drawl, an exaggerated fear of ghosts, a singular disability to use big words correctly, and with a noticeably lazy or shiftless manner. On radio, the portrayal of black people did little to disrupt the culture of prejudice. One well-known personality featured a supporting performer in the role of valet and chauffeur. Although the portrayal was sympathetic, it was scarcely flattering to Negroes. At least one radio play remained popular among whites for years by mimicking two black persons and a group of their associates. These characterizations were actually performed by whites. This series, in effect, defined the black community as peopled mainly by knaves, simpletons, and ne'er-do-wells. It was all very funny—except if you happened to be black.

Organized agitation eventually forced removal of such offensive material from the content of mass communication. Before long, the purge extended to a number of ethnic and nationality groups. Thus, the villains of today are a remarkably Americanized lot. We no longer see Italian gangsters on our screens, or Poles, or Jews, or anyone else with identifiable racial or ethnic characteristics cast in unsympathetic roles. Anyone who plays a "heavy" these days is given a Midwestern accent and a name no more sinister than Smith. No cruel Fu Manchu sends shivers down the backs of contemporary audiences; no Charlie Chan solves crimes with fractured English and quaint Oriental sayings. Even the Nazis have been made into warm and lovable characters in at least one current TV play about a German prison camp! Only the Russians seem to remain the "dirty guys." If international relations improve, presumably even they will join the side of the angels.

Recognizing the grossly discriminating employment practices in the communications industry prevailing until the last year or so, the industry is now bringing black announcers, actors, models, and other personnel into the nation's mass communications. Perhaps at some future time the continued appearance of such people on our television screens and in our magazines and movies will suggest to white people that black people are really part of our society. Such communications, in other words, may alter the definition of the situation so that skin color will become a less significant variable in human interaction than it is at present.

On the other hand, these efforts on the part of the mass media are rather minor elements in the complex equation which governs the relationship between dominant and minority segments of the society. Prejudice and discrimination, after all, have been part of our society since its beginning. It may be entirely too simplistic to expect that the presence or absence of black faces or Italian accents on our TV screens will have much to do with the reduction of racial or ethnic discrimination on the part of the majority. The culture of prejudice and norms of discrimination remain in full force among the dominant group. They are as much a part of the lessons the ordinary citizen learns while growing up as how to button his clothes and eat with a knife and fork. Prejudice and discrimination, in other words, are supported by deeply institutionalized folkways, mores, and values. They are a *de facto* and central part of the American way of life, like Motherhood and the Flag. Therefore, there is a powerful argument against those who would have us believe that the media can convert us into correcting these shortcomings in our democratic system. This begins with the simple fact that the American public is intensely preoccupied with its media. The argument goes on to note that these media stress democratic lessons daily and nightly. But in spite of this schooling, we remain essentially a nation in which socially approved bigotry is common. If the media were that powerful, we would be practicing brotherhood instead of only preaching it for others.

Overall, this somewhat confusing normative theory of mass communication influence seems to sum up in something like the following terms: The media can *reinforce* cultural norms, as they do every day, and thus indirectly play a part in shaping conduct along established lines. They can undoubtedly *activate* a considerable amount of behavior, providing it is consistent with the needs of the individual and socially approved within the existing structure of cultural norms. (The classic case here is the Kate Smith marathon radio broadcasts which sold 15 million dollars' worth of war bonds in a single day.)[27] The media can even *create* new norms in areas of behavior which are not currently controlled by strong sociocultural constraints. It remains much in doubt, however, that the media alone have any effective power to *convert* populations from one form of conduct to another by changing definitions of the situation among the relevant actors. It seems clear, in other words, that the media do not *change* deeply institutionalized norms and thereby significantly alter conduct. These conclusions, like most others about the media, are tentative and subject to change on the basis of convincing data.

The cultural norms theory has in recent years assumed a rather curious role in international politics. American involvment in Vietnam has touched off some of the most vigorous debate the country has seen in recent years. Protest groups have attempted to gain the limelight, which a news-hungry communications industry has eagerly granted them, through a variety of demonstrations of every kind. Underlying these efforts seems to be the conviction on the part of the demonstrators that the public at large will somehow be persuaded to take the point of view of the demonstrators. The exact linkage between the publicity given to the acts of militant or other dissident groups and potential changes in normative public attitudes is not at all clear. One could just as easily hypothesize that such publicity would creat negative reactions as well as positive. In fact, the "boomerang" effect is a well-understood phenomenon in mass communications research. Nevertheless, the idea that they are achieving persuasion toward their point of view appears to be popular among those who stage public demonstrations to gain media coverage.

Another role of unknown but potentially great significance that the cultural norms theory plays in international politics is the possible creation of a "definition of the situation" among groups with whom the country currently happens to be at odds. At certain points in the Paris negotiations the North Vietnamese, for example, were said to have been guided in their interpretations of what public opinion was doing in the United States by the content of the news media concerning objections to the war. When protest groups gained media coverage, goes one interpretation, this made it appear as if the majority of people in the United States supported the view presented by the dissenters. Whether this charge was true, or whether the North Vietnamese based policy on such data, will only be revealed by future historians who analyze the records of these events. At present all we can say is that if someone who knew very little about the American society attempted to develop an understanding of its people on the basis of news media alone, he would reach some rather bizarre conclusions. For example, he would be led to believe that we spent our time mainly in killing each other with automobiles, setting fire to each other's buildings, committing crimes, showing adulation to sports and entertainment figures, and arguing about politics. In other words, there is much popular mythology surrounding the social norms theory. In general it appears to be accorded a much more powerful role in manipulating publics than it probably deserves.

Another area in which the cultural norms theory has become central to current controversies is the impact of the high levels of violence in the content of our movies, television, and other media. Even the most casual observations would lead one to suspect that these media are portraying violence with great frequency. These suspicions have been repeatedly confirmed by systematic research. Recently, for example,

Gerbner has undertaken for the President's Commission on the Causes and Prevention of Violence to assess the level of violence appearing in ordinary television drama. To do this, he analyzed all of the content of two typical weeks of TV fare from the three major networks. Of *all* programs presented, more than 80 percent contained violence in some form![28] Turning to dramatic plays, such as spy thrillers, westerns, and detective stories, he found that 455 leading characters had appeared on the screen in these broadcasts during the time period studied. "By the end of the plays, 241 committed some violence, 54 killed an opponent and 24 died violent deaths . . . A count of visible casualties revealed an average of five per play injured or dead."[29]

This adds up to a lot of violence in two weeks. Over a number of years, these figures would be astronomical. "One report to the Federal Communications Commission stated that between the ages of 5 and 14 the average American child has witnessed the violent destruction of 13,000 human beings on television alone."[30]

But what do all of these scary statistics mean? What is all of this violence doing to us—if anything? Expert opinion is totally deadlocked as to whether exposure to such violent portrayals is harmful or beneficial. A number of laboratory experiments imply that a subject who has been frustrated prior to seeing portrayed violence has a higher probability of engaging in violence himself if the opportunity arises.[31] Other research, seemingly equally valid, indicates that viewing portrayed violence results in a *cathartic* effect; it actually reduces the subsequent probability that the subject will perform violent acts.[32] As yet, this issue is very much an open one, and it is not possible to draw final conclusions from the available research.

One thing is certain, however, and that is that in spite of their enjoyment of vicarious violence, Americans continue to disapprove overwhelmingly of serious violence in reality. They do this in spite of the massive doses of mayhem that they have been receiving for years via their media. Their norms in reality, in other words, are quite at odds with those implied by media content. Even the use of violence by the police is not sanctioned indiscriminately by the public: "The majority of Americans approve of police use of violence only when the provocation is illegal and potentially threatening to the life of the policeman or directly hindering law enforcement."[33]

Thus, American norms concerning violence, like those of smoking and prejudice, remain virtually *undisturbed,* even in the face of intense media preoccupation with this type of content. How long this will remain a stable situation is hard to say. Anti-violence norms are at least as deeply rooted in the American culture as those of any other form of behavior. Furthermore, unlike smoking and discriminating, they are given almost *universal social approval,* both by the overwhelming majority of ordinary people and by official institutions of the society. Because of this, there is probably far less danger that we are all going to become violent toward each other because we watch TV than many alarmists would have us believe. Frightening statistics about what appears on the screen, or impressive numbers about how many million people watch how many zillion hours of television, do not necessarily translate into actual changes in deeply established cultural norms. Therefore, it need not follow that TV is slowly converting our normally law-abiding citizenry into a weakly controlled mob ready at any moment to fly into a rage of aggression and violence. Elementary historical observation indicates that the overwhelming majority of citizens are not now any more violent than they were at an earlier time. In fact, if one reviews the general social conditions that prevailed in the society from which contemporary American life has emerged, there is a good case to be made that we are much less violent today than we were earlier. Television obviously played no part in such affairs as the Whiskey Rebellion, the New York draft riots during the Civil War, the shoot-out at the O.K. Corral, the reign of John Dillinger, the thousands of lynchings in the South, and so on. Even the troublesome upheavals of ghetto and campus violence that have plagued us recently have stemmed from more basic causes than what their participants have seen on TV, in the movies, or in *Time* magazine.

One of the problems in reviewing this issue objectively is that each generation of intellectual critics seems determined to use the media as scapegoats for trends which they find disquieting in their society. The newspapers of the 19th century were roundly condemned for "causing crime" when they reported crime news. Later, the movies of the early 1930's were said to "cause delinquency." [34] Comics were bitterly attacked in the 1950's as a direct stimulant to youthful misconduct.[35] Television now seems to be bearing the brunt of the attack.

Another problem in discussing the issue of media violence is that many critics of the media are apparently unable to separate their personal opinions about the esthetic merits of media content from objective conclusions reached from relevant data. Many highly educated persons, including social scientists involved in the debate over media effects, find much media content to be offensive to their tastes and a disappointment to their hopes for a better mankind. Thomas P. F. Hoving, Director of New York's Metropolitan Museum of Art, puts it this way:

There is in man, most of us would like to think, the capacity or at least the aspiration for bettering himself, his family, his community, his nation, his world. How often, rising in disgust after the hours wasted in front of the TV, have we thought of any such hopes or goals.[36]

Such comments are typical of the "frustrated hopeful," as El-Assal has called the critic who believes that the media really do have the power to better the world, but who also believes that the bad men in charge are deliberately withholding their benefits from us.[37] Such conclusions lead the critic to think of those in charge of the media in such terms as (to quote Mr. Hoving) ". . . ghouls who prey on the American spirit in the hopes of increasing their soapsud and dog food sales." [38] Usually, the message of the critic contains the implicit prescription that if the media would only adopt the esthetic norms and humanitarian values that they, the critics, hold, then the world would be all right. Violence, for example, seems especially objectionable in any form. Because of such feelings, it seems to follow that portrayals of violence are bound to be doing harmful things to the people who view them. Certainly, as one critic has recently posed the issue, the media cannot readily demonstrate that this is *not* happening. Therefore, the argument runs, the media must be condemned.[39]

The fact that such arguments beg the question and confuse feelings with evidence leads some students of the media to object to them, just as they object to confused logic and polemics leading to any other conclusion. However, such objections run the risk of being labeled as from persons who are either gullible or in the pay of the media. This debate, in short, is one carried on at a high level of emotional tension, and one where pleas for objectivity are largely ignored. One may generally upbraid the media for pandering to the tastes of the least common denominator, and object strenuously to the use of media time for presenting frivolous or offensive material when there are so many important things that they could do. However, to conclude that such outcries constitute reliable evidence on the relationship between mass communication and some type of effect is simply nonsense. If any individual enters the arena of this debate and wishes to be taken seriously, he must make his case on the basis of evidence about which independent analysts can agree. Thus far, such evidence is not available. In all likelihood, therefore, intellectual critics will continue to try, condemn, and (attempt to) execute the media on the basis of their own values. An obvious, but perhaps less attractive, alternative for them would be to do the difficult research that would yield the needed facts.

Overall, then, the cultural norms theory remains as one of the least tested, most controversial, and potentially most significant of contemporary theories of mass communication. A monumental task lies ahead for communications specialists and other social scientists in discovering the factors, limitations, and conditions under which the media have the power to shape norms and, in turn, indirectly mediate individual human conduct. As these become increasingly clear, the intensity of the debate over the cultural norms theory will undoubtedly decline.

MODELS OF THE PERSUASION PROCESS

The foregoing theories of the way in which mass communication content influences individual conduct have led to numerous attempts to capitalize on these conceptualizations for the purpose of deliberately manipulating human behavior by mass communicated messages. The massive efforts of the advertising world are one obvious example. Perhaps equally obvious are public-service campaigns that attempt to persuade people to engage in a variety of socially approved behaviors. Again obvious is the case of political persuasion, where the voting act is the object of continuing efforts to manipulate behavior with communication content.

The relationship between contemporary theories of mass communication and conceptualizations of how persuasion can be achieved is not a straightforward one. The world of advertising is perhaps more of an art than an activity based upon scientifically formulated theories. The same is true of other forms of persuasion. However, analyses of contemporary persuasion campaigns reveal certain regularities, certain significant similarities, in their apparent *underlying assumptions* about how the persuasion process works. These assumptions can be formalized into two rather broad "models" of the persuasion process which are described below.

In attempting to describe the nature of these formulations, two things will be quite clear. First, these models of the persuasion process (which is simply another way of talking about a "theory" of how it works) are *extensions* and *utilizations* of the contemporary theories of mass communication that have been reviewed in the present chapter. Second, these models are *roughly formulated* at the present time. Perhaps even a third point will suggest itself; there are undoubtedly a number of other models of the persuasion process that could be formulated as alternatives.

The first of these two conceptualizations can be called the *psychodynamic* model of the persuasion process. It is based almost exclusively upon what we have termed the "individual differences theory" of mass communication effect. Although one of the first theories of mass communication to be recognized, the individual differences theory remains an important one. This is revealed by the impact that it has had upon the advertising and public relations world. It has also provided the principal set of assumptions underlying much social-psychological research on persuasion in recent years.

The essence of the idea is that an effective persuasive message is said to be one which has properties capable of *altering the psychological functioning* of the individual in such a way that he will respond overtly (toward the item that is the object of persuasion) with modes of behavior desired or suggested by the communicator. In other words, it has been assumed that the key to effective persuasion lies in modifying the internal psychological structure of the individual so that the psychodynamic relationship between latent internal processes (motivation, attitudes, etc.) and manifest overt behavior will lead to acts intended by the persuader.[40]

There have been many specific forms or variants of this persuasion model, depending upon the particular psychological phenomena under study, and upon the presumed dynamic relationships thought to prevail between the psychological process and the overt behavior patterns that they supposedly activate. Extensive use has been made of persuasive messages aimed at individual attitudes or opinions under the assumption that there is a close relationship between a person's attitudinal structure and the way he behaves in overt social situations.[41] A common example would be the type of mass communication campaign aimed at reducing ethnic discrimination (overt behavior) by attempting to reduce ethnic prejudice (psychological process purported to lead to discrimination). Another example would be an attempt to promote the purchase of a patent medicine (overt action) by instilling a fear of poor health or continued suffering (psychological process). The general idea could be illustrated with examples ranging from chest X-ray drives and charity appeals to anti-litterbug campaigns and political oratory. Among the many psychological concepts that have been used intervening variables are sexual urges, status drives, desires for social approval, anxieties, fears, vanity, and a host of others. In simple graphic terms, the *psychodynamic model* of the persuasion process would be as follows:

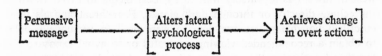

As has already been implied, this persuasion model is backed by impressive experimental evidence. An extensive social-psychological literature has accumulated with respect to many variables thought to be potentially useful as modifiers of overt action.[42] One major research group has even concluded that there are some people who come already structured as "persuasible types" so that their resistance to psychological manipulation is lower than that of the ordinary person, regardless of the item of persuasion or the psychological basis of the appeals.[43]

The psychodynamic model rests upon an extensive theoretical as well as empirical base. Important theories of motivation, perception, learning, and even psychoanalysis have suggested ways in which attitudes, opinions, fears, self-conceptions, perceptions of source credibility, reinforcement, and many other variables are related to persuasion. In fact, some studies among this accumulated literature have been so widely quoted and reprinted that the rather tentative nature of the original conclusions is in danger of being forgotten. But wide quotation or reprinting is not equivalent to wide replication. Further evidence is needed to support the psychodynamic model of persuasion. Systematic and valid assertions are needed as to which variables under what circumstances can be used to manipulate what kind of people toward what patterns of action when messages incorporating those variables are brought to their attention. Not only is the evidence as yet incomplete concerning the utility of this approach to persuasion, but those who employ this strategy sometimes make unrealistic assumptions. For example, some experimentalists have been willing to assume that if their communication was demonstrably able to change attitudes or opinions, then patterns of overt behavior would be correspondingly changed. Such an assumption is unwarranted. Festinger has reviewed relevant literature on this problem.[44]

But the fact that the validity of the psychodynamic model of the persuasion process has as yet not been fully verified does not mean that it is incorrect. It does seem to work some of the time. For example, during a recent eclipse of the sun, the population of a Midwestern town was repeatedly warned by local media to avoid viewing the eclipse directly or through dark glasses. Fear-threat appeals that described possible severe eye damage were used to persuade people to obtain a recommended viewing apparatus or to avoid exposure altogether by viewing the event on television. A study conducted immediately following the eclipse indicated that there was a positive relationship between the amount of fear aroused in a given recipient of those messages and his degrees of overt compliance.[45]

In contrast, an earlier experimental study of somewhat parallel fear-threat messages directed toward groups of high school students showed the reverse. Illustrated lectures showing damage to teeth as a result of improper dental hygiene were presented to several groups of subjects. An inverse relationship between fear-threat compliance was found. Those who received the strongest fear-threat showed the least compliance with the preventive program advocated by the communicator. Those experiencing the least fear-threat showed the most compliance. The results of this well-controlled and frequently quoted study were exactly the opposite of those from the study of the eclipse.[46] Such seemingly opposite findings in the case of two variants of a fear-threat-health campaign point emphatically to the need to sort out the conditions under which a given psychodynamic variable will lead to a particular type of action and when it will "boomerang" and suppress it.

The same can be said of the individual differences theory in general. There are many kinds of "effects" other than overt adoption of some action advocated in persuasive messages. Children learn new ideas and practices from the media through a process of *incidental learning*.[47] This may be totally unrelated to the intent of educators or persuaders. People may take up new habits, adopt new fads, change their musical tastes, or bolster their loyalty to a political party without complying in any sense to a persuasive message deliberately directed toward them. While the individual differences theory suggests that variations in their personality structures will play an important part in determining the manner in which this happens, it would be incorrect to say that a fully articulated theory is now available explaining the role of such factors. At the same time, an impressive array of research findings show how *some* individual characteristics do play *some* part in determining the kind of effect that a given message content will have on a particular type of person. These studies along with many others have recently been reviewed and imaginatively discussed by Klapper.[48] He points up vigorously the need to consider many other variables besides individual personality characteristics in developing theories of the effects of the media, and the dangers inherent in constructing simple cause-effect types of theory. This is a point of view with which we heartily agree. The present chapter treats several theories in cause-effect terms because it is attempting to show the *development* of mass communication theory over time as well as its broad scope.

In 1948, Bernard Berelson attempted to summarize the status of the field of mass communication as it then existed. He noted that the older theory of the all-powerful media had largely been abandoned, and he identified five central factors that seemed to be the focus of research at the time:

> Now, in the 1940's, a body of empirical research is accumulating which provides some refined knowledge on the effect of communication on public opinion and promises to provide a good deal more in the next years.
> But what has such research contributed to the problem? . . . The proper answer to the general question, the answer which constitutes a useful formulation for research purposes, is this: Some kinds of *communication* on some kinds of issues, brought to the attention of some kinds of *people* under some kinds of *conditions,* have some kinds of *effects.*[49]

This set of propositions may have been short of being a tightly formulated theory of mass communication, but it clearly rested upon the kinds of assumptions which we have called the individual differences theory. If faced with the need to predict the probable impact of a given type of communication on a given issue, and where the "conditions" of communication (radio, print, etc.) are understood or controlled, the major variables not manipulatable by the communicator are the "kinds of people." In other words, a communicator who was able to select his message and his issue, and by-and-large structure the conditions of communication as he wished, still had no direct control over his audiences' prejudices, predispositions, amount of prior information, etc. Thus, the independent variables (messages on a given issue presented under known conditions) are modified in their impact on the dependent variables (effects) by the action of intervening variables ("kinds of people," i.e., individual differences in relevant psychological variables).

The Berelson formulation quoted above did, however, elaborate on the elementary form of the individual differences theory by calling specific attention to the fact that variations in the stimulus material and variations in the social setting or other related conditions as well as in the psychological structures of members of the audience could be expected to have an impact upon the kinds of effects produced. In spite of its simplicity, it did serve as a guide for research, a kind of general statement of the salient groups of factors and variables, which along with individual differences, must be considered in trying to understand the communication process.

While the individual differences theory of mass media effects led to the formulation of the "psychodynamic model" of the persuasion process in attempts to use the theory for practical purposes, this model has by no means been the only one that has been tried. A somewhat more complicated alternative stems from a combination of the social relationships theory and the cultural norms theory. For the lack of a better term, we will refer to this as the *sociocultural model* of the persuasion process.

Little systematic theory has emerged from the experimental literature on persuasion regarding the use of sociocultural variables as a basis for appeals in persuasive communication. Social and cultural variables have been widely recognized by communications researchers and other social scientists as playing an important part in determining the way in which people adopt new ideas and things. But the way in which such variables can be deliberately incorporated into messages to facilitate persuasion has not received much attention. In fact, existing theories of persuasion, and of the adoption of innovation, see group, interactional, and cultural variables mainly in terms of *obstacles* to achieving persuasion or adoption.[50] The reason for this may have been the almost overwhelming preoccupation with the psychodynamic model that has already been discussed.[51]

Much basic research in behavioral science indicates that what we are terming sociocultural variables are very important sources from which individuals gain definitions of appropriate behavior in a group context. They are, as we will indicate in greater detail, important sources from which the individual derives *interpretations of reality* as well as being significant froms of *social control*.[52] The body of basic research on such issues spans the social sciences from anthropology to sociology. In addition to studies of culture such as those of Ruth Benedict, laboratory experiments such as those of Asch and Sherif show how even in the simplest and most artificial setting, the influence of *norms* plays a powerful role in guiding, defining, and modifying the behavior of the individual, somewhat independently of the state of his internal predispositions.[53] Sociological studies have supported this generalization. The work of Lohman and Reitzes,[54] Minard,[55] Newcomb,[56] De Fleur and Westie,[57] Gorden,[58] Merton and Kitt,[59] and Mead,[60] indicate the way in which such variables as *organizational membership, work roles, reference groups, cultural norms,* and *primary group norms* can play a part in shaping and channeling overt action in ways that are to some extent uninfluenced by internal psychological predispositions. At the very least, it must be recognized that the behavior patterns of a given individual can seldom be accurately interpreted on the basis of individual psychological variables *alone,* particularly when the individual is acting within a socal context. To explain, predict, or manipulate such behavior, reference must be made to the social norms, roles, social controls, and culturally defined or shared values, expectations, and beliefs, which surround action, in order that it can be effectively understood.

The sociocultural processes present in a given individual's situation of action, then, are important determiners of the directions that such action will take, or indeed whether action will occur at all. These actions can even be contrary to individual predisposition, although certainly this is not the general case. The more frequently occurring situation would be where sociocultural variables modify the way in which psychological processes give rise to overt action.

The sociocultural model of the persuasion process suggested from these considerations is based upon the assumption that mass communicated messages can be used to provide an individual with new and seemingly group-supported interpretations of some phenomenon toward which the individual is acting. By so doing, it may be possible to mediate the conduct of the individual as he derives definitions of appropriate behavior and belief from such suggested interpretations. Even in cases where individual predispositions run contrary to the suggested action, it may be possible to obtain compliance by suggesting to the individual a set of social and cultural constraints to which he feels compelled to conform. An even simpler situation would be where the individual has not yet formulated strong psychological predispositions one way or the other toward the object of persuasion.

In such a case, he would hold few group-derived definitions of appropriate action toward it. Under such conditions, suggested definitions would pose little social or psychological conflict in following the modes of action prescribed by the communicator. Represented schematically, such a model of the persuasion process looks something like this:

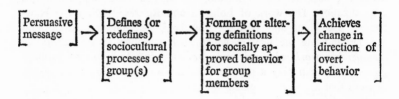

But what are the means by which groups provide the individual with "sanctioned" or "approved" modes of conduct toward objects, events, or issues which are brought to the individual's attention? This apparently takes place in many ways. Such concepts as *roles, norms, shared values, status,* and *social control* are some of the elements in the "definitions of situations" that are culturally provided for individuals acting in social settings. These group-derived definitions of situations specify modes of orientation toward a wide variety of objects and events toward which responses must habitually be made. These modes of orientation constitute an important part of the institutionalized subcultural patterns of groups. With respect to innovations, or new ideas, beliefs, or things of any kind, groups and societies vary widely in the degree to which stable, institutionalized rules exist "ready-made" for orienting the individual toward new phenomena. Margaret Mead has described societies having rigid and deeply institutionalized cultures that provide the individual with a ready-made "reality" against which to interpret any new phenomenon. Other societies are at the other extreme, where the individual is on his own to construct modes of reaction to new events on the basis of his own internal processes.[61] The American society apparently lies somewhere between these two extremes. Each individual is a member of groups that are of significance to him, but at the same time the culture is sufficiently complex, contradictory, and heterogeneous so that modes of reaction to new issues are not uniformly prescribed.

We may suggest, then, that anthropological, psychiatric, social-psychological, and sociological evidence indicates clearly that one of the main functions of groups is to provide shared orientations for members by means of which they can interpret realities to which they as individuals have only limited direct access at best. Realities are defined and interpreted within social frameworks. This generalization has often been called the *reality principle,* and the interactional process by means of which such definitions are achieved has been referred to as *consensual validation.*

These two concepts have bearing on the present conceptualization in that it is suggested the *persuasive messages presented via the mass media may provide the appearance of consensus with respect to a given object or goal of persuasion.* That is, such messages can present definitions to audiences with respect to innovations in such a way that the listener is led to believe that these are the socially sanctioned modes of orientation toward such objects in groups that are of significance to him. The communicator provides social realities, shortcutting the process of consensual validation, particularly with respect to objects or practices concerning which groups do not yet have fully institutionalized cultural interpretations, or in the case where such interpretations are not contrary to the goals of the persuasion.

In specific terms it can be suggested that the communicator can stress the way in which a specific *role* is defined (so as to include the use of the object of persuasion). Such messages can demonstrate how adoption of the communicator's goal is *normative* in the group within which this role lies. The communicator can show how the nonadopter is a *deviant* and a *nonconformist* (in the negative sense). The way in which negative *social sanctions* are brought to bear upon such deviants and nonconformists may be clarified. At the same time, the manner in which *social rewards* and *social approval* are given to the adopter of the communicator's goals may be stressed. Finally, the manner in which adoption achieves *group integration,* and how such behavior is consistent with *group approved values,* can be brought out.

To illustrate in concrete terms the actual use of the sociocultural model as a strategy for persuasion, we may examine the tactics used by certain types of charity drives, commonly called "United Appeals," "Community Funds," and so forth. Such persuasive campaigns make use of both the psychodynamic and the sociocultural models of the persuasive process. As will be seen, they not only use mass communications as part of their tactics but other types of messages as well.

For the sake of emphasis, we will assume a hypothetical individual who is not particularly sympathetic to this form of campaign, preferring to make his donations to his favorite charity instead. As we will see, however, in spite of his contrary internal predisposition, he has little chance of resisting. For reasons which will be made clear, it is very likely that he will be persuaded to make a donation.

The first step in the campaign is an announcement (via the mass media) that the community has a specific *quota* which must be met by the drive. Thus, a goal is defined with the suggestion that this has widespread approval in the community. This goal has been arbitrarily formulated by the organizers of the drive, of course, and not necessarily from grass-roots sentiment on the part of the community members. However, it is very likely to go unchallenged. Goals have a rather compelling quality in themselves if it is believed that they have group support (consensus). Such an impression can be created by getting socially eminent persons in the community to participate in the announcement of the quota. The mass media will always obligingly give full coverage to such an event and thereby confer status upon it.

Another significant step is to announce to the community that the "fair share" of each citizen is some specified percent of his weekly earnings. This concept will also be given ample coverage by the media. The idea of a "fair share" is sociologically meaningful. It is compelling to the individual because it seems to be an approved and shared *norm*. Who wants to be identified as "unfair," and thus *deviant* from approved values? If our imaginary individual is led to believe that others are giving according to this norm, he will at least feel some pressure toward conformity.

At the heart of the persuasion campaign is the task of creating *role systems* that are linked to the fund drive within work groups in the community. In stores, factories, schools, and as many other organizations as possible, a "chairman" for the drive is appointed with attendant publicity. Leaders of such organizations feel compelled to cooperate in this because of the need to maintain appearances that the organization operates in the interest of the public. The chairman usually appoints sub-chairmen for various divisions of the organization if it is at all large. The rank and file member of the group must play a *counter-role* to the roles of these collectors within their work setting. When asked personally by a fellow worker—especially the boss's secretary—it is difficult to refuse a donation.

Another tactic in this sociocultural strategy is to prepare and distribute to each member an IBM card with his name on it and with a place to mark how much he is "pledging" (to be collected later). The person who chooses not to pledge anything must publicly signify his deviancy by signing the card to indicate refusal, or by telling the chairman of his group personally that he will not make a donation.

If our hapless individual, who really wanted to give his funds to another worthy cause, has not been persuaded by these strategies, he will be confronted with an even more compelling situation when he gets home. The organizers of the campaign appoint "volunteer collectors" who will call on residents in their immediate area and request a donation. Here we have the role of *neighbor* and that of *good citizen* (which includes charity) locked into a reciprocal system in miniature. It is socially embarrassing to refuse a neighbor a reasonable and socially approved request. Potential negative sanctions underlie such refusal. Who wants to be known to his neighbor as such a tightwad that he would refuse to donate a modest sum to an important charitable cause. Therefore, our friend at this point reaches into his pocket for some folding money, and possibly grits his teeth a little while he smilingly conforms. However, for his capitulation to social pressure he will be given positive reinforcement. He will get a little button to wear in his lapel, which will help indicate to others the nature of the approved norms.

With the skillful use of the media, therefore, plus the use of social norms, roles, and social controls in real ways, such campaigns can be very successful. The variables utilized give the potential donor an unmistakable "definition of the situation" and place him within a set of sociocultural constraints that are nearly impossible to ignore. While this rather complex illustration of sociocultural strategy does not use mass communications exclusively, they occupy a central place in the activities of the persuaders. In other adaptations of this strategy, the entire persuasive effort might be handled by the media alone. If there is any doubt that this strategy is widely used, the reader is invited to spend an evening before his TV set viewing commercials within the perspective of the sociocultural strategy. The smiling and happy people who act out their little dramas concerning cigarettes, beer, laxatives, deodorants, and denture paste are offering a most fascinating variety of "definitions of the situation."

There are undoubtedly numerous other ways in which persuasion processes could be conceptualized. The psychodynamic and the sociocultural strategies, however, seem to have rather clear links to the theories of mass communication effects that have been discussed in the present chapter.

THE FUTURE OF MASS COMMUNICATION THEORY

One of the most pressing problems in the interdisciplinary study of mass communication is the strengthening of its theoretical base. There has been an unfortunate tendency among students of the media to equate the idea of "theory" with relatively unsophisticated matters such as classification schemes, the preparation of abstract diagrams that purport to symbolize the communication process, or the mere listing of factors that somehow "make a difference" in the way some communication effect takes place. Criteria of what constitutes a theory in more sophisticated fields are considerably more demanding. In a very real way, the four contemporary theories of mass communication that have been discussed in the present chapter reflect these limitations. For reasons that will be discussed, they are not truly theories at all. They are relatively simple formulations that have been given easy-to-remember names for purposes of convenience. In reality, these conceptualizations did not emerge full-blown from research in precisely the way they have been discussed, but they have been implicit in debates, writing, and research for years.

In terms of implications for the future, there remain two major problems associated with the four theories that have been reviewed. First, they are in certain respects "dead ends." Mass media researchers seem to have lost interest in some of these conceptualizations altogether and they are at a complete standstill as far as further development is concerned. The individual differences theory, for example, remains as valid now as it was at any time when its essential propositions were being drawn from research. Yet, with minor exceptions, no one is now attempting to uncover further generalizations about how psychological variables such as needs, attitudes, cognitive habits, etc., play a part in producing given effects among media audiences. Much of the same can be said about the social categories theory. Interest subsided some time ago in discovering how broad uniformities among people, in terms of age, sex, ethnicity, or other variables, lead to certain uniformities of response to mass communicated messages. The idea that interest has declined because we know all there is to know about such matters can be dismissed at once. We have barely begun to assemble truly reliable, systematized, and complete knowledge on such issues.

In the case of the social relationships theory, the discovery that variables related to mass communication effects were also related to the adoption of innovation and social change in a broader sense has apparently worked to the detriment of mass communication theory. The social scientists that did the basic work on the social relationships theory became so enamored with more general issues bearing on the diffusion of innovation that they dropped further work on the media and concentrated their efforts on the adoption process itself.

The cultural norms theory is a slightly different matter. Only now is real interest being shown in the idea, and that largely because certain political figures discovered that violence and delinquency made excellent political issues. The cultural norms theory has been with us for many years, but as yet no one has attempted to formalize it, test it thoroughly, and set forth its areas of applicability or limitation in a systematic manner. In other words, the development of mass communication theory has been at the mercy of fads and fashions as these have waned and waxed among students of the media, critics, or political figures. There has been more waning than waxing in recent years with respect to some theories. To some extent the lack of continued dedication to fundamental theoretical problems related to the media may be a product of the history of mass communication as a field of research and study. Until recently, it has been little more than a kind of intellectual way-station—a kind of unclaimed territory where people from all kinds of disciplinary backgrounds have come in, picked up research problems, worked through them for a while, and then dropped them in favor of more pressing interests or pursued their implications back into the main stream of their own discipline. Perhaps as communication continues to develop into a discipline in its own right, with its own research training and a growing conceptual apparatus, it will increasingly be able to concentrate on the systematic accumulation of theories of mass communication.

A second major problem related to these contemporary theories has already been suggested; namely that if considered within a framework of more rigorous criteria they are scarcely theories at all. This is not to discount their validity—an issue that will be settled in the arena of research—but to point to the fact that they are oversimplifications, and vaguely stated ones at that. They need to be completely revamped and rewritten as systematic sets of propositions that show in straightforward terms just what is supposed to be related to what in terms of independent and dependent variables. To do this, some very difficult definitional work will have to be undertaken so that the exact phenomena to which the concepts in the theories refer can be identified. Relationships between concepts within given propositions will have to be identified by means of some logical *calculus*—some set of recognized rules for reasoning—so that orders of dependencey between propositions can be established. If this is done, such theories will yield *derived propositions* that can be tested empirically. Only then can their validity be adequately assessed.

This does not mean that all of mass communication theory must be reduced to algebraic equations. These steps are possible without resorting to mathematics. However, it is one thing to state propositions like this: "ideas often flow from the media to opinion leaders and from them to less active populations." It is quite another thing to specify precisely what quantitative relationships are meant by such terms as "often" and "less," and to note exact empirical referents for other terms in such a statement, such as "ideas," "flow," "leaders," etc. In other words, we must more rigorously specify the conditions under which these events will occur, in what quantity or with what probability, and with what step-by-step theoretical implications for related media behavior.

This call for raising scientific standards in media research implies that students of mass communication have a great deal of homework to do before they can increase the sophistication of their theoretical formulations to the level of other disciplines. There is a serious gap between what we *think* we know about how mass communication effects take place and a rigorous set of theoretical formulations that specify how they *actually do* take place. In other words, there is a need to establish increased confidence that these basic theories are true (or else replace them) and thereby increase the degree to which we can discuss cause-effect sequences in mass communication in precise terms. Until the formulations identified in the present chapter have been studied, restudied, reformulated, and restudied again many times over, they will remain forever as "pre-theories"—interesting and seemingly plausible speculations that appear to be more or less consistent with our limited amount of research on the effects of mass communication but about which we really are not sure.

As our research technology becomes more effective, for example, as such tools as the computer make it easier to handle larger and larger complexes of variables, the probability that we will come up with true theories of mass communication effects seems increasingly high. One obvious approach would be to *combine* the four theories that have been discussed in the present chapter. Such an *integrated* theory would recognize that the effects of a given mass communicated message sent over a given channel will depend upon a large number of psychological characteristics and social category similarities among the members of the audience; these effects will depend upon the kind of social groups within which these people are acting and the relationships that they have with specific types of persons within them; they will depend upon the social norms that prevail among such groups in reality as well as upon the "definitions of the situation" which the communicated messages are to suggest. Perhaps when it is possible to pin down some of these variables in specific detail, we can truly develop theories of mass communication.

In overview, the present chapter has attempted to show the dependent relationship between general theoretical development in the basic social and behavioral sciences and the more specific formulations that have emerged from mass communication research concerning the effects of the media. As psychologists increasingly recognized individual variations in learning, perception, motivation, and other psychological processes, the older mechanistic theory of mass communication (which postulated uniform response to communication stimuli) became untenable. The idea of individual differences in response to the mass media was quickly incorporated into communications research. At the same time, sociologists continued to identify behavioral uniformities among significant social categories in the urban-industrial society, and this idea was applied to the study of mass communication audiences. Later, the continuous "rediscovery" of the primary group in the midst of what was thought to be a strictly "mass" society finally led to the discovery of the significance of social relationships in the mass communication process. These relationships became the focus of intense interest by students of the media. Finally, the recognition of the place of social norms in human life has been central to sociological and anthropological theory since the 19th century. Such norms have long been a rather controversial part of thoughtways concerning mass communication.

In general, then, it appears that there is a relationship of dependency between the basic social and behavioral sciences and more specialized fields such as the study of mass communication. This should come as no surprise. However, there is one final comment that can be made concerning this relationship. The linkage between such fields in terms of theoretical development is not a simple and straightforward one. The specialized field can move forward on its own without waiting for broader developments; similarly, the specialized field can lag badly behind basic theory. In fact, it is quite possible that the order of dependency could be reversed in some cases. For example, sociologists have had to rethink their basic theories of the structure of contemporary society because of findings concerning the significant presence of primary groups—findings that have emerged from just such areas as mass communications research. In any case, the theories (or "pre-theories") and their limitations, which have been discussed in the present chapter, represent our present point of development in the task of understanding how mass communications affect the members of populations who attend to them.

Chapter VIII

MASS MEDIA AS SOCIAL SYSTEMS

WHILE THE mass communication research and theory of the recent past and of the contemporary period has almost uniformly stressed "effects" as the major object of explanation, it has been repeatedly suggested in the present volume that there are other, and possibly equally important, aspects of the media that deserve theoretical and empirical attention. One of the most challenging of such issues concerning these media is their ability to *survive* and for long periods of time provide their audiences with content which the more artistically sensitive elite has regularly condemned as being in bad taste or even downright dangerous. There has been a continuous dialogue carried on between the more educated and conservative elements of society and those who are either in control of the media or who serve as their spokesmen. This issue of "elite culture" vs. "mass culture" has on some occasions stirred debate in the highest political, educational, religious, and legal circles of the nation. A long series of court battles has been fought over books, magazines, and other forms of print which their publishers claim are "artistic" but which public prosecutors maintain are "pornographic." Attempts to censor motion pictures at the community and state levels have also provided occasions for extensive legal actions. The freedom of speech principle vs. statutory prohibitions of lewd, lascivious, or salacious portrayals provide ample grounds for lively discussion. Even the Congress of the United States periodically enters this controversy when it investigates television content, comic books, or other media to determine if they are causally related to juvenile delinquency or cause some other form of deviant conduct.

In these encounters, the media seldom or never emerge unscathed. At the very least, they nearly always evoke strong criticism. Whether the situation is a formal hearing before a congressional committee, or simply the reflections of some well-known literary figure giving his views on the worth of media content, the ordinary fare of the mass media of communication has been universally and roundly condemned by society's political, educational, and moral leaders.

Such hostility has deep historical foundations. Plato may have provided the opening round in the controversy long before the mass media themselves were ever invented. In his commentary on the training of the children who were to become the leaders of his ideal Republic, he saw the mass culture of his day as posing a threat to the minds of the young:

> Then shall we simply allow our children to listen to any stories that anyone happens to make up, and so receive into their minds ideas often the very opposite of those we shall think they ought to have when they are grown up?

> No, certainly not [replies Glaucon].

> It seems, then, our first business will be to supervise the making of fables and legends, rejecting all which are unsatisfactory; and we shall induce nurses and mothers to tell their children only those which we have approved. . . . Most of the stories now in use must be discarded.[1]

This theme—popular entertainment is harmful to the minds of the young—has been a consistent one from the very beginnings of mass communication. It has been claimed from time to time that such charges can be validated by scientific evidence, but repeatedly this evidence has turned out to be less than convincing.[2] Social scientists insist that any important conclusions about the effects of the media be supported by solid evidence. Because of such insistence upon data rather than emotion, they sometimes find themselves in the awkward position of seeming to defend the media when actually they are simply refusing to accept the inadequately supported claims of critics. Most social scientists today are quite wary of any simple answers or unverified conclusions concerning causal relations between media content and undesirable conduct.

However, the insistence that conclusions be based upon adequate evidence has never deterred the literary critic from charging the media with a deep responsibility for society's problems. Most 19th century

American writers at some point in their careers took time to criticize and condemn the newspaper for superficiality and distortion. The following excerpts from the pens of well-known and influential literary figures are samples of the climate of opinion prevailing among the literati during the time when the mass newspaper was diffusing through the American society:

Henry David Thoreau (written just prior to 1850):

The penny-post is, commonly, an institution through which you seriously offer a man that penny for his thoughts which is so safely offered in jest. And I am sure that I have never read any memorable news in a newspaper. If we read of one man robbed, or murdered, or killed by accident, or one house burned, or one vessel wrecked, or one steamboat blown up, or one cow run over on the Western Railroad, or one mad dog killed, or one lot of grasshoppers in the winter—we never need read of another. If you are acquainted with the principle, what do you care for a myriad instances and applications? To a philosopher all news, as it is called, is gossip, and they who read it and edit it are old women over their tea.[3]

Thomas Carlyle (written about 1860):

But indeed the most unaccountable ready-writer of all is, probably, the common editor of a Daily Newspaper. Consider his leading articles; . . . straw that has been thrashed a hundred times without wheat; ephemeral sound of a sound; . . . how a man buckles himself nightly with new vigor and interest to this thrashed straw, nightly thrashes it anew . . . this is a fact remaining still to be accounted for in human physiology.[4]

Samuel Clemens (written in 1873):

That awful power, the public opinion of this nation, is formed and molded by a horde of ignorant self-complacent simpletons who failed at ditching and shoemaking and fetched up in journalism on their way to the poorhouse.[5]

Stephen Crane (written about 1895):

A newspaper is a collection of half-injustices
Which, bawled by boys from mile to mile,
Spreads its curious opinion
To a million merciful and sneering men,
While families cuddle the joys of the fireside
When spurred by tale of lone agony.

A newspaper is a court
Where everyone is kindly and unfairly tried
By a squalor of honest men.

A newspaper is a market
Where wisdom sells its freedom
And melons are crowned by the crowd.

A newspaper is a game
Where his error scores the player victory,
While another's skill wins death.

A newspaper is a symbol;
It is a feckless life's chronicle,
A collection of loud tales
Concentrating eternal stupidities,
That in remote ages lived unhaltered,
Roaming through a fenceless world.[6]

As each of the remaining media arrived on the American scene, they too were denounced for their assault on the morals and intelligence of the nation, or at least for bringing about a deterioration of public taste. The motion picture, popular music on radio, comic books, and of course violence on television have all been the subject of accusation, claim, and counterclaim.

But in spite of the intensity of this exchange, and in spite of the respectability, power, and authority of those who have been most vocal in their criticisms, the media continue year after year to deliver to their audiences the same popular and superficial fare! There may be minor fluctuations in the acceptability to the elite of the content of a particular medium during any given period, but in the long run, from their point of view, media content is showing no impressive indications that it is raising its cultural level.

The *tenacity* and *stability* of the mass media generally in the face of such a long history of criticism by powerful voices needs explanation. The problem at first seems deceptively simple. One tempting answer is that the media appeal to the masses and the masses want the kind of content they get and so the media continue to give it to them. Such a conclusion is, of course, correct as far as it goes, but it does not account for the relative ineffectiveness of the critics, who are often, in fact, persons of substantial influence. Unfortunately, also, it is tautological as well as superficial, and it is more a description than an explanation.

A promising approach to understanding the relationship between mass media content and public taste, and for accounting in part for the remarkable continuity in the (low) cultural level of media content is provided by viewing the media as *social systems* which operate within a specific external system—the set of social and cultural conditions that is the American society itself.

General sociological theory has become increasingly preoccupied with the nature of social systems. Of particular interest are the functional relationships prevailing between parts of such systems, and the consequences that particular items occurring within the system have in maintaining the stability of the system as a whole. In certain respects, this rise of interest in the analysis of social phenomena as occurring within the boundaries of social systems represents a renewal of interest in the theoretical strategies of the past. A more complex terminology has replaced the outmoded organic lexicons of Spencer and Ward, but there remain many similarities between the sociological analyses of the two periods.

One of the major dissimilarities, however, is that the analysis of social systems concerns itself with the *patterns of action* exhibited by individuals or subgroups who relate themselves to each other within such systems. (The older organic analogies were less specific.) A social system is, for this reason, an *abstraction*—but one not too far removed from the observable and empirically verifiable behaviors of the persons who are doing the acting.

The actions of any given human being generally follow the expectations imposed upon him by the cultural norms of his society and of those who interact with him. Cultural norms, then, in the form of the expectations regarding conduct that people in a group have of each other, are an inseparable part of a social system in reality. Yet, by concentrating not upon such expectations, but upon the visible conduct of people attempting to *fulfill* these expectations, stable systems of social action can be mapped out, various parts or components of such systems can be identified, and the contributions toward stability made by a given repetitive form of action in a system can be inferred, and hopefully, verified.

We might add that it is clearly recognized that individual human beings who are acting out their roles within a system (or any other stimulus field) have internal feelings, thoughts, attitudes, and other value-orientations that are in some part determinants of their action. These internal psychological behaviors in reality play important parts in shaping the manner in which individual actors in a given system of action play out their parts. However, within a particular social system (a given family, community, factory, etc.) the range of variation of these psychological influences cannot be too great or the system would disintegrate. As one leading group of social scientists has put it:

Indeed, one of the most important functional imperatives of the maintenance of social systems is that the value-orientations of the different actors in the same social system must be integrated in some measure in a *common* system. All ongoing social systems do actually show a tendency toward a general system of common cultural orientations. The sharing of value-orientations is especially crucial, although consensus with respect to systems of ideas and expressive symbols are also very important determinants of stability in the social system.[7]

The social system, then, is a complex of stable, repetitive, and patterned action that is in part a manifestation of the culture shared by the actors, and in part a manifestation of the psychological orientations of the actors (which are in turn derived from that culture). The *cultural system,* the *social system,* and the *personality systems* (of the individual actors) therefore, are different kinds of abstractions made from the same basic data, namely, the overt and symbolic behaviors of individual human beings. They are equally legitimate abstractions, each providing in its own right a basis for various kinds of explanations and predictions. Generally speaking, it may be difficult or nearly impossible to analyze or to understand fully one such abstraction without some reference to the others.

But, granted that the term "social system" is a legitimate scientific abstraction, how does this general conceptual strategy help in understanding the mass media of communication? To answer this question, we need to understand in greater detail exactly what is meant by the term social system, and what type of analysis it provides. To aid in providing such understanding we turn briefly to several ideas that are important aspects of the study of social systems. One of the most important of these ideas is the concept of the "function" of some particular *repetitive phenomenon* (set of actions) within such a system. For it was with questions about a particular repetitive phenomenon (the continuous production and distribution of media content in "low" cultural taste) that the present chapter began. The fact that such content has long survived the jibes of influential critics was said to require explanation. One form of explanation will be provided by noting the "function" of such a repetitive phenomenon within some stable system of action. The term "function" in the present context means little more than "consequence." To illustrate briefly, we might hypothesize that the repetitive practice of wearing wedding rings on the part of a given married couple has the function (consequence) of reminding them as well as others that the two are bound together by the obligations and ties that matrimony implies. This practice thereby contributes indirectly to maintaining the permanance of the marriage—the stability of that particular social system. The practice is in a sense "explained" by noting its contribution to the context within which it occurs. A comparison of a number of such systems with and without this particular item (but in other respects matched) would test the assertion.

In the above example, the social system is a relatively simple one. There are only two "components," and each of these happens to be an individual. Their patterns of action are derived both from the individual psychological make-up of the partners and from the cultural norms concerning marriage prevailing in their community, social class, and society. It is a miniature system in equilibrium, although it would not remain long in equilibrium unless the "needs" of the system remained satisfied. For example, such a system requires that the partners perform roles that meet the expectations each has of the other and the expectations the community has of married couples. This can be thought of as a "need" for adequate role performance, without which the equilibrium of the system would be endangered. Other "needs," related to economic matters and emotional satisfactions, could be cited.

More complex illustrations of social systems can easily be pointed to, where the "components" of the system are not individual persons, but subsystems. A department store, for example, is a complex social system consisting of the actions of managerial personnel, buyers, sales persons, the clerical staff, customers, transportation workers, stock boys, a janitorial team, and security employees. Each of these components is a smaller system of action within the broader system of the store itself, and it in turn is a complex system of action carried out within the context of the external social conditions of the community. In spite of the complexity, any given set of repetitive actions might be analyzed in terms of their contribution to maintaining the system in equilibrium, or even as contributing to its disequilibrium. The granting to employees of the right to buy merchandise at cost could have the function (consequence) of maintaining their morale and loyalty, and thus such behavior would contribute fairly directly to the maintenance of the system. Rigid insistence on the observance of petty rules, such as docking the pay of an employee who on rare occasions was late for work, might be disruptive of such morale and loyalty, and by contributing to labor turnover it could be *dysfunctional*. Instead of contributing to the maintainance of the system, it could cause disruptions and disequilibrium. Such inductively derived conclusions would be subject to testing for validity, of course, but the functional analysis would have generated the hypothesis to be tested (an important role of theory).

A "functional analysis," then, focuses upon some specific phenomenon occurring within a social system. It then attempts to show how this phenomenon has consequences that contribute to the stability and permanence of the system as a whole. The phenomenon may, of course, have a negative influence, and if so, it would be said to have "dysfunctions" rather than "functions." The analysis is a strategy for inducing or locating hypotheses that can be tested empirically by comparative studies or other appropriate research methods.

The analysis of social systems is extremely difficult. In fact, this strategy for the study of social phenomena is at the forefront of general sociological theory. There are no infallible rules that specify precisely how to locate and define the exact boundaries of a given social system, particularly if it is relatively complex. There are as yet no completely agreed upon criteria for establishing the linkages between the components of a system, and there are no standard formulae for uncovering the precise contribution that a given repetitive form of action makes to the equilibrium of a system. A functional analysis of the contribution of some item to the stability of a system, then, is a procedure that is somewhat less than completely rigorous. But in spite of this source of potential criticism, this strategy for studying and understanding complex social phenomena seems to hold a great deal of promise.

The basic logic of functional analysis has been described by Hempel with clarity and precision:

The object of the analysis is some "item" i, which is a relatively persistent trait or disposition ... occurring in a system s ...; and the analysis aims to show that s is in a state, or internal condition, c_i and in an environment presenting certain external conditions c_e such that under conditions c_i and c_e (jointly referred to as c) the trait i has effects which satisfy some "need" or "functional requirement" of s, i.e., a condition n which is necessary for the system's remaining in adequate, or effective, or proper, working order.[8]

How can this type of analysis be applied to the mass media? First, as has been suggested in the previous paragraphs of the present chapter, the portion of the content of the mass media that is in "low" cultural taste or provides gratifications to the mass audience in such a manner that it is widely held to be potentially debasing can be defined as "item i" (in Hempel's terms, above). It is fully recognized that there are very serious problems with such a conceptualization right at the beginning. It would be difficult in practice to construct a *set of categories* under which to analyze the content of the media so that material of "low" cultural taste can readily be identified. It would be difficult, but actually it would not be altogether impossible. Excessive violence, the portrayal of criminal techniques, horror and monster themes, open pornography, suggestive music, and dreary formula melodramas are typical categories of content that arouse the ire of critics. There would probably be considerable disagreement as to the exact content that should be included in any given category. There would also be debates over the number of categories to be used. Nevertheless, it is theoretically possible to identify the content of any given medium that is *most* objected to by the largest number of critics.

We will not actually carry out the exercise for the purposes of the present discussion. However, we will assume that given sufficient time and resources, and using survey techniques, preference scales, attitude measuring instruments, and other research procedures now available that the content of any given medium could be divided roughly into something like the following three categories:

low-taste content: This would be media content widely distributed and attended to by the mass audience, but which has consistently aroused the ire of critics. Examples would be crime drama on television which emphasizes violence, openly pornographic motion pictures, daytime serials, confession magazines, crime comics, suggestive music, or other content that has been widely held to contribute to a lowering of taste, disruption of morals, or stimulation toward socially unacceptable conduct. (Whether or not such charges are true.)

nondebated content: This would be media content, widely distributed and attended to, about which media critics have said very little. It is not an issue in the debate over the impact of the media on the masses. Examples would be television weather reports, some news content, music that is neither symphonic nor popular, many magazines devoted to specialized interests, motion pictures using "wholesome" themes, and many others. Such content is not believed either to elevate or lower tastes, and it is not seen as a threat to moral standards.

high-taste content: This would be media content sometimes widely distributed but not necessarily widely attended to. It is content that media critics feel is in better taste, is morally uplifting, educational, or is in some way inspiring. Examples would be serious music, sophisticated drama, political discussions, art films, or magazines devoted to political commentary. Such content is championed by critics as the opposite of the low-taste material, which they see as distinctly objectionable.

It is, of course, to the *first* of the above categories that we wish to direct most of our attention. This will constitute the "item i" in the logical scheme outlined by Hempel. It is the repetitive phenomenon whose contribution to the media (as a social system) needs analysis. However, it would also be possible to study the other two categories with somewhat parallel perspectives, but this will receive relatively little attention in the present discussion.

Having focused upon the repetitive "item i," we need now to begin to identify the boundaries of the social system within which this phenomenon occurs, so that eventually the contribution it makes to the system can be inductively hypothesized.

Rather than developing a purely descriptive scheme that will apply only to a single medium, it will be more fruitful to attempt to develop a *general* conceptual scheme into which any or all of the media could be placed, with suitable minor modifications in details. Such a general scheme will emphasize the similarities between media, particularly in terms of relationships between the components in the system. If the same general regularities appear to prevail between the parallel components of several media in much the same way, such a conclusion would suggest that such regularities constitute a *class* of events that follows patterns occurring naturally, given the conditions under which they have been arranged. This, of course, opens the door for explanatory analyses—the inductive construction of hypotheses. The first step in the development of explanatory theory is the location of classes of events that seem to occur in much the same way, given the presence of specified conditions. This, indeed, may point to the value of a functional analysis, where events are viewed as occurring within social systems. Such a functional analysis itself is not a theory, nor is the description of an abstract social system a theory. This approach is a strategy of investigation that hopefully will identify classes of events and the ways they are related to each other in systematic linkages. These can then become the *explicanda* of deductive nomological theories that are capable of "explanation" in the more rigorous sense.[9]

The first major component of the social system of mass communication is the *audience*. As has been suggested in previous chapters and as is perfectly clear from elementary observation, this is an exceedingly complex component. The audience is stratified, differentiated, and interrelated in the many ways which social scientists have studied for years. The several theories, previously discussed, indicate some of the major variables that play a part in determining how this component will operate within the system.

The individual differences theory, the social categories theory, the social relationships theory, and the cultural norms theory all point to behavioral mechanisms that determine the patterns of attention, interpretation, and response of an audience with respect to content of a given type.

The rough typology of content suggested earlier in the present chapter is in some degree related to the characteristics of this audience. Organizations devoted to *research,* to measuring the preferences of media audiences, or to various forms of market research provide information to those responsible for selecting the categories of content that will be distributed to the audience. There is a link, then, between the audience as a component in the system and the market research-rating service organizations as a second component. In purely theoretical terms, both components are role systems themselves, and are thus actually subsystems. This is in a sense a one-way link. For very minor (or usually no) personal reward, the audience member selected for study provides information about himself to such an agency. Information flows from the audience component to the research component, but very little flows back. This linkage between components is by comparison relatively simple.

The content itself, of whatever type, flows from some form of *distributor* to the audience. The role system of the distributor component varies in detail from one medium to another. In addition, there are several somewhat distinct subsystems within this general component. First, there are local outlets, which are likely to be in the most immediate contact with the audience. The local newspaper, the local theater, the local broadcasting station play the most immediate part in placing messages before their respective audiences. But inseparably tied to them are other subsystems of this general component. Newspaper syndicates, broadcasting networks, or chains of movie theaters pass content on to their local outlets. The link between these two subsystems is a two-way one. The local outlet provides money and the larger distributor supplies content. Or, the linkage may be that the local outlet

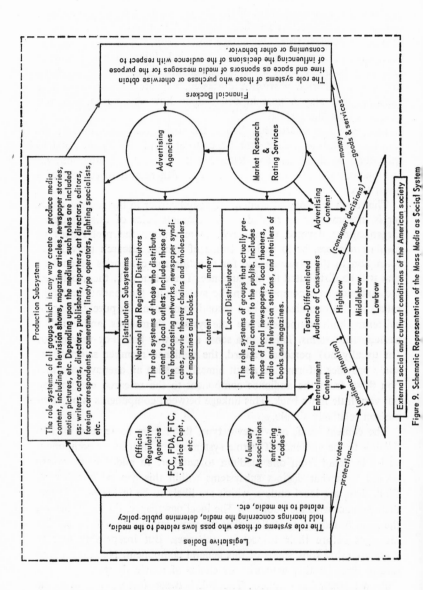

Figure 9. Schematic Representation of the Mass Media as Social System

Production Subsystem

The role systems of all groups which in any way create or produce media content, including television shows, magazine articles, newspaper stories, motion pictures, etc. Depending upon the medium, such roles are included as: writers, actors, directors, publishers, reporters, art directors, editors, foreign correspondents, cameramen, linotype operators, lighting specialists, etc.

Distribution Subsystems

National and Regional Distributors

The role systems of those who distribute content to local outlets: Includes those of the broadcasting networks, newspaper syndicates, movie theater chains and wholesalers of magazines and books.

Local Distributors

The role systems of groups that actually present media content to the public. Includes those of local newspapers, local theaters, radio and television stations, and retailers of books and magazines.

Advertising Agencies

Market Research & Rating Services

Financial Backers

The role systems of those who purchase or otherwise obtain time and space as sponsors of media messages for the purpose of influencing the decisions of the audience with respect to consuming or other behavior.

Official Regulative Agencies
FCC, FDA, FTC, Justice Dept., etc.

Voluntary Associations enforcing "codes"

Legislative Bodies

The role systems of those who pass laws related to the media, hold hearings concerning the media, determine public policy related to the media, etc.

Taste-Differentiated Audience of Consumers

Highbrow

Middlebrow

Lowbrow

Advertising Content

Entertainment Content

content

money

money & services

goods & services

(consumer decisions)

(audience attention)

votes

protection

— External social and cultural conditions of the American society —

provides a service, and the distributor (who is paid elsewhere) provides money.

The relationship between audience and distributor seems at first to be mostly a one-way link. The distributor provides entertainment content (and often advertising), but the audience provides little back in a direct sense. However, it does provide its *attention*. In fact, it is precisely the attention of the audience that the distributor is attempting to solicit. He sells this "commodity" directly to his financial backer or sponsor. In addition, as we have noted, the audience supplies information to the research component and this is indirectly supplied to the distributor in the form of feedback so that he may gauge the amount of attention he is eliciting. The linkages between components grow more complex as we seek the boundaries of the system.

To the audience, the research, and the distributing components, we may add the role system of the *producer* of content. This component's primary link is with the *financial backer* (or *sponsor*) component and with the distributor, from whom money is obtained and for whom various forms of entertainment content are manufactured. There are a host of subsystems included in this producer component, depending upon the particular medium. Examples are actors, directors, television producers, cameramen, technicians, foreign correspondents, wire service editors, film producers, labor union leaders, publishers, copy editors, clerical staff and many, many more.

Linking the sponsor, distributor, producer, and research organization are the *advertising agencies*. Paid primarily by the sponsor, this component provides (in return) certain ideas and services. For the most part, it provides the distributor with advertising messages. It may have links with the research component as well.

Over this complex set of interrelated components, there are other subsystems that exert *control*. The legislative bodies, at both the state and national level, which enact regulative statutes concerning the media, constitute an important part of such a control component. Another important part of this role subsystem is the official regulative agencies, which implement the policies which have been legislated. The link between the legislative body (control component) and the audience is of course one of votes and public opinion, to which the component is presumably sensitive and dependent. Information lines between audience, legislative bodies, and regulatory agencies are more or less open.

To the regulatory components whose role definitions are found in legal statute can be added the private voluntary associations that develop "codes" and to some degree serve as a control over the distributors. Such distributors provide them with money, and they in turn provide surveillance and other services.

The regulatory subsystems draw definitions of permissible and nonpermissible content from the general set of *external conditions* within which this extremely complicated system operates. Surrounding the entire structure as an external condition are our society's general norms concerning morality, and the expressions that these find in formal law. Similar, although less likely to be incorporated into law, are our general cultural norms and beliefs regarding what will be likely to entertain or otherwise gratify Americans. Thus, we seldom see traditional Chinese opera, but frequently see western horse opera. We seldom hear the strains of Hindu temple music, but frequently hear the "strains" and other noises of the latest singer whom teen-agers admire. If our interests run to more serious fare, we are likely to hear the music of a relatively small list of European or American composers who created their works within a span of about three centuries. Or, we are likely to view ballet, opera, drama, etc., of a fairly limited number of artists whose products are defined by our society as of lasting interest.

Each of the several media will fit into this general model of a social system in slightly different ways. A complete description of each of the media separately would be tedious. Indeed, each could well occupy the contents of an entire book. Opotowsky has attempted just such a detailed analysis of the television industry, although he does not use the social system concept.[10]

To add to the complexity of this conceptual scheme, it must be remembered that although each medium constitutes a somewhat separate social system in itself, the media are also related *to each other* in systematic ways. Thus, we may speak of the entire set of communication media, including those which have not been specifically analyzed in the present volume, as the mass communication system of the United States.

The structure of this mass communication system has been heavily influenced by the general social, political, economic, and cultural conditions that were current during the period when our mass media were developing and remain as important sociocultural forces in the society within which they operate. Due to their importance for understanding our media as they are today, these conditions were analyzed in some detail in earlier chapters. Our free enterprise beliefs, our views of the legitimacy of the profit motive, the virtues of controlled capitalism, and our general values concerning freedom of speech constitute further *external conditions* (in addition to those related to moral limits and cultural tastes) within which the American mass communication system operates.

Within the system itself, the principal *internal condition* is, of course, a financial one. Most of the components in the system are occupational role structures, which motivate their incumbent personnel primarily through money. To obtain money, they are all ultimately dependent upon the most central component of all—the audience. Unless its decisions to give attention, to purchase, to vote, etc., are made in favorable ways, the system would undergo severe strain and would eventually collapse.

Almost any dramatic change in the behavior of the audience would cause the most severe disruption in the system for any given medium. In an earlier chapter, the swift acquisition of television sets by the movie audience was plotted (Figure 4). The consequence of attention loss to the motion picture theater as a mass medium was shown to be severe (Figure 2).

Such disruptions are infrequent, but they do occur. The key to heading off dramatic changes in audience behavior, of course, is to provide entertainment content of a type that will satisfy and motivate the largest possible number of audience members to carry out their roles in accord with the needs of the system. Such content will, in other words, *maintain the equilibrium of the system*. The ideal, from the standpoint of the system, is content that will capture the audience member's attention, persuade him to purchase goods, and at the same time be sufficiently within the bounds of moral norms and standards of taste so that unfavorable actions by the regulatory components are not provoked.

The type of entertainment content that seems most capable of eliciting the attention of the largest number of audience members is the more dramatic, low-taste content. Films, television plays, newspaper accounts, or magazine stories that stress physical violence, brutality, sexual gratification, earthy humor, slapstick, or simple melodrama appeal most to those whose educational backgrounds are limited. Their prior socialization has not provided them with sensitive standards for appreciation of the arts or for judging the cultural, educational, or moral merits of a given communication within complex frameworks. In the affluent American society, it is this type of audience member who is by far the most numerous. He has purchasing power in sufficient abundance so that his combined influence on the market can be overwhelming. He is in full possession of the media. He subscribes to a daily paper, has several radio receivers, and owns a television set. He also goes to the movies occasionally. In fact, there are ample data showing that he spends considerably *more* time with the media than his more educated and possibly more affluent fellow citizen. While the college graduate in the middle or upper-middle class is going to a concert, having a bridge party, or attending a play, the family with considerably less education and lower occupational status is happily enjoying a popular comedian or a variety show on their television set. Furthermore, there are about five times as many of the latter type of family for every one of the former. Not only are they considerably more numerous, but they all use laundry detergent, toothpaste, deodorants, gasoline, cigarettes, and beer in the same amount or perhaps to an even greater degree per family as the more well-to-do. In short, they are the most numerous units in the market, units whose tastes must be catered to if the system is to survive. The manufacturer of razor blades who sells millions of his product per day to American men does not care at all if his customer has a college degree or is nearly illiterate. If he shaves and can be persuaded to buy the manufacturer's blades via mass communicated advertisements, this is all the manufacturer requires. If it takes a western melodrama filled with blood and thunder to attract the consuming unit's attention to the advertisement, so be it. If that small segment of the population who are highly educated or who have refined tastes do not find the end result culturally uplifting, that is just too bad. If they want culture let them go to the opera. If they turn on their television sets, they had better be prepared to listen to advertisements about razor blades *and* the vehicles that can bring them to the attention of the most massive number of consuming units. No matter what the critics say, these are the elementary facts of economic life within which the American mass communication system operates.

What we have called low-taste content is the key element in the social system of the media. It keeps the entire complex together. By continuously catering to the tastes of those who constitute the largest segment of the market, the financial stability of the system can be maintained. The critic who provokes public attention by denouncing media content or by proclaiming that there is a causal connection between media content and socially undesirable behavior may temporarily receive some recognition. He may also achieve some temporary disturbance in the system, or if he is persistent enough he may ultimately even displace some specific form of low-taste content from a given medium altogether. Thus, if quiz shows are found to be "rigged," or if popular "disc jockeys" are discovered receiving "payola" (a fee for repeatedly playing a song in order to make it popular) the audience may be temporarily disaffected. However, low-taste content comes in such a variety of forms that the temporary or even permanent absence of one minor form does not alter the major picture. Critics have been complaining about newspaper concentration on crime news for a century, and there has been no noticeable abatement in the reporting of such stories. Critics of the soap opera may have breathed a sigh of relief several years ago when these programs at last disappeared from radio. However, their joy must have been short-lived when such day-time serials turned out to be quite popular with television viewers, so popular in fact that one even occupied a place in prime evening hours for several years.

When a formula is discovered for eliciting attention and influencing purchasing decisions from any large segment of the audience, it will be abandoned by the media only with great reluctance, if at all. The broadcast ball game, the star comedian, the family situation comedy, the western thriller, the detective story, the adventures of the private investigator, the drama of the courtroom now are beginning to rank with such time-honored formulae as the sob story, the funnies, the sex-murder account, the sports page, and the disclosure of corruption in high places, as attention-getting devices that can bring the eye or ear of the consumer nearer to the advertising message.

In short, the social system of the mass media in the United States is becoming more and more deeply established. Some future changes can be expected in the kind of content which it will produce to maintain its own equilibrium, but these will be slow in coming and minor in nature. As the educational level of the average citizen slowly rises in our society, there is some prospect that his tastes will change. On the other hand, as standards of sexual morality become increasingly liberal, the tastes of a slightly more educated mass audience may still demand increasingly frank portrayals in film and television drama. Standards of other types may change or fail to change in equally complex ways.

At present, however, the function of what we have called low-taste content is to maintain the financial equilibrium of *a deeply institutionalized social system which is tightly integrated with the whole of the American economic institution.* The probability that our system of mass communication in this respect can be drastically altered by the occasional outbursts of critics seems small indeed.

In the present volume the mass media have been viewed from a considerable variety of theoretical perspectives, and in each case it was suggested that there was a close link between the general theories of the more basic social sciences and the interpretations students of communication have given of the media. As these general images of man have changed, so have theories of mass communication. To some it may appear that a considerable inefficiency of effort is involved. This may be true. But hopefully, these changes, revisions, and new directions have not been simple random variations. Bit by bit, the development of theory in mass communication, with a corresponding accumulation of supporting empirical evidence, will enable us to understand better how societies influence their media, how the communicative act takes place via the mass media, and how mass communication content influences the members of society.

NOTES

CHAPTER II

1. Eric Barnouw, *Mass Communication* (New York, Rinehart and Company, Inc., 1956), p. 7.
2. For an excellent summary of functions of mass communication today, including "surveillance," see Charles R. Wright, *Mass Communication: A Sociological Perspective* (New York, Random House, Inc., 1959), pp. 17–23.
3. Edwin Emery and H. L. Smith, *The Press and America* (New York, Prentice-Hall, Inc., 1954), pp. 415–416.
4. See for example: H. Earl Pemberton, "The Curve of Culture Diffusion Rate," *American Sociological Review*, Vol. I, No. 4 (August, 1936), pp. 547–556; Stuart C. Dodd, "Diffusion Is Predictable: Testing Probability Models for Laws of Interaction," *American Sociological Review*, Vol. 20, No. 4 (August, 1955), pp. 392–401; Everett M. Rogers, *Diffusion of Innovations* (New York, The Free Press of Glencoe, 1962), pp. 152–159.
5. The following two research studies bear directly on this point: Bernard Berelson, "What Missing the Newspaper Means," in P. F. Lazarsfeld and F. N. Stanton, eds., *Communications Research, 1948–1949* (New York, Harper and Brothers, 1949), pp. 111–129; Penn Kimball, "People Without Papers," *Public Opinion Quarterly*, Vol. 23, No. 3 (Fall, 1959), pp. 389–398.

CHAPTER III

1. Martin Quigley, Jr., *Magic Shadows; The Story of the Origin of Motion Pictures* (Washington, D.C., Georgetown University Press, 1948), pp. 18–20.
2. Helmut Gernsheim and Alison Gernsheim, *The History of Photography From the Earliest Use of the Camera Obscura in the Eleventh*

Century Up to 1914 (London, Oxford University Press, 1955). See especially Chapter I, "The History of the Camera Obscura," pp. 1–19.

3. Martin Quigley, Jr., *op. cit.*, pp. 29–35.
4. A reproduction of this famous work has recently been made available. See John Baptista Porta, *Natural Magick*, Derek J. Price, ed. (New York, Smithsonian Institute for Basic Books, Inc., 1957).
5. *Ibid.*, pp. 364–365.
6. Martin Quigley, Jr., *op. cit.*, pp. 48–61.
7. *Ibid.*, pp. 85–97.
8. Josef M. Eder, *History of Photography* (New York, Columbia University Press, 1945), pp. 209–245, 263–264, 316–321.
9. Robert Taft, *Photography and the American Scene* (New York, The Macmillan Company, 1938), p. 3.
10. *Ibid.*, p. 48.
11. *Ibid.*, pp. 55–62.
12. *Ibid.*, p. 76.
13. *Ibid.*, pp. 384–404.
14. Martin Quigley, Jr., *op. cit.*, see especially Chapters XV and XVI.
15. Richard Griffith and Arthur Mayor, *The Movies* (New York, Simon and Schuster, Inc., 1957), pp. 1–8.
16. *Ibid.*, p. 19.
17. *Ibid.*, pp. 113–119.

CHAPTER IV

1. Gleason L. Archer, *History of Radio to 1926* (New York, The American Historical Society, Inc., 1938).
2. John Baptista Porta, *op. cit.*
3. Monroe Upton, *Electronics for Everyone*, 2d rev. ed. (New York, American Library Association, 1962), p. 137.
4. S. G. Sturmey, *The Economic Development of Radio* (London, Gerald Duckworth and Company, Ltd., 1958), p. 17.
5. Gleason L. Archer, *op. cit.*, p. 91.
6. *Ibid.*, pp. 112–113.
7. Gleason L. Archer, *op. cit.*, p. 312.
8. Girard Chester, Garnet R. Garrison, and Edgar Willis, *Television and Radio*, 3rd ed. (New York, Appleton-Century-Crofts, 1963), p. 24.
9. Alfred N. Goldsmith and Austin C. Lescarboura, *This Thing Called Broadcasting* (New York, Henry Holt & Company, Inc., 1930), p. 279.
10. John F. Seggar, Cyrus Johnson, and Lyle Warner, "Mass Media Ownership Among Appalachian Low Income Families" (forthcoming), University of Kentucky.
11. Robert Rees *et al.*, "The Uninformed; Media-Isolated Farm Families In Four Appalachian Counties" (forthcoming), University of Kentucky.

CHAPTER V

1. Charles A. Kofoid *et al.*, eds., *Termites and Termite Control* (Berkeley, University of California Press, 1934), p. 8.
2. *Ibid.*, p. 11.

3. A. M. Guhl, "The Social Order of Chickens," *Scientific American,* Vol. 194, No. 2 (February, 1956), p. 43.

4. *Ibid.,* p. 43.

5. George Herbert Mead, *Mind, Self and Society* (Chicago, University of Chicago Press, 1934). This work is the principal source for the theoretical approach of the present chapter.

6. A recent statement on the importance of symbolic interaction theory in social psychology can be found in: Arnold Rose, ed., *Human Nature and Social Processes* (Boston, Houghton Mifflin Company, 1962).

7. These include: Claude E. Shannon and Warren Weaver, *The Mathematical Theory of Communication* (Urbana, University of Illinois Press, 1949); George A. Miller, "The Idealized Communication System," *Language and Communication* (New York, McGraw-Hill Book Company, Inc., 1951), pp. 6–8; Wilbur Schramm, "How Communication Works," *The Process and Effects of Mass Communication* (Urbana, University of Illinois Press, 1954), pp. 3–26; plus many others. A review of relevant literature is contained in Melvin L. De Fleur and Otto N. Larsen, *The Flow of Information* (New York, Harper and Brothers, 1958).

8. The study of internal meaning responses has received far less attention from psychologists than the importance of the problem might suggest. The most important research in recent decades is that of Charles E. Osgood and associates. This outstanding and imaginative line of research is reported in Charles E. Osgood, George J. Suci, and Percy H. Tannenbaum, *The Measurement of Meaning* (Urbana, University of Illinois Press, 1957). It was from this source that a number of ideas were drawn for the present analysis of the communicative act.

9. The sources of noise, its characteristics and consequences, are important research problems for several of the sciences.

CHAPTER VI

1. Bernard Berelson, "The State of Communication Research," *Public Opinion Quarterly,* Vol. 23, No. 1 (Spring, 1959), pp. 1–17.

2. Auguste Comte, *The Positive Philosophy,* trans. by Harriet Martineau, Vol. II (London, George Bell and Sons, Ltd., 1915), p. 289.

3. *Ibid.,* p. 292.

4. *Ibid.,* p. 293.

5. *Ibid.,* p. 293.

6. Herbert Spencer, *The Principles of Sociology* (New York, D. Appleton and Company, 1898), pp. 452–462.

7. Ferdinand Tönnies, *Community and Society (Gemeinschaft und Gesellschaft),* trans. and ed. by Charles P. Loomis (East Lansing, The Michigan State University Press, 1957), p. 47.

8. *Ibid.,* p. 65.

9. Emile Durkheim, *The Division of Labor in Society,* trans. by George Simpson (New York, The Free Press of Glencoe, 1964).

10. *Ibid.,* pp. 62–63.

11. *Ibid.,* p. 129.

12. *Ibid.,* p. 130.

13. *Ibid.*, p. 131.
14. *Ibid.*, p. 137.
15. *Ibid.*, p. 206.
16. *Ibid.*, p. 353.
17. *Ibid.*, p. 361.
18. See, for example, the well known treatment of the "mass" by Herbert Blumer, which is still regarded as the classic modern statement of the concept: Herbert Blumer, "Elementary Collective Behavior," Alfred McClung Lee, ed., *New Outline of the Principles of Sociology* (New York, Barnes and Noble, Inc., 1939), pp. 185–189.
19. Leonard Broom and Philip Selznick, *Sociology,* 2d ed. (Evanston, Illinois, Row, Peterson & Company, 1958), p. 38. The quotation within the passage is from: Kimball Young, *Sociology* (New York, American Book Company, 1949), p. 24.
20. Ferdinand Tönnies, *op. cit.,* p. 47.
21. George Sylvester Viereck, *Spreading Germs of Hate* (New York, Horace Liveright, Inc., 1930), pp. 153–154.
22. Harold D. Lasswell, *Propaganda Technique in the World War* (New York, Alfred A. Knopf, Inc., 1927), pp. 220–221.
23. Elihu Katz and Paul Lazarsfeld, *Personal Influence* (Glencoe, Illinois, The Free Press, 1954), p. 20.
24. Harold D. Lasswell, *op. cit.,* p. 221.
25. Katz and Lazarsfeld point out that both those who feared the media as potentially insidious devices if controlled by evil men and those who hailed them as beneficial means to improve democracy were assuming a similar great degree of media power. See: Elihu Katz and Paul Lazarsfeld, *op. cit.,* pp. 15–17.

CHAPTER VII

1. Examples of such works are: Bernard Berelson, *Content Analysis In Communication Research* (Glencoe, Illinois, The Free Press, 1952), and Gilbert Seldes, *The American Audience* (New York, The Viking Press, 1950).
2. Otto N. Larsen, "Social Effects of Mass Communication," Robert E. L. Faris, ed., *Handbook of Modern Sociology* (Chicago, Rand McNally & Company, 1964), p. 348.
3. There are several possible explanations for this frequent failure to look beyond effect. First, the early "mechanistic S-R" theory of mass communication concentrated upon effect. Second, financial support for studying this "practical" problem is far easier to obtain than for more "theoretical" questions. Third, there has been a high level of popular interest in effects and therefore a more ready audience for publications dealing with them.
4. William James, *Principles of Psychology* (New York, Henry Holt and Company, 1890). See p. 566.
5. John B. Watson, *Behavior: An Introduction to Comparative Psychology* (New York, Henry Holt and Company, 1914).
6. Although the basic idea of conditioning was understood before the turn of the century, it was the work of physiologists such as Ivan

Pavlov and Vladimir Bekhterev that made it popular among American psychologists. An excellent discussion of this historical development is that of Ernest Hilgard and Donald Marquis, *Conditioning and Learning* (New York, Appleton-Century-Crofts, 1940), esp. pp. 1–50.

7. For an outstanding overview of development during this period of thought concerning human personality, see: Gordon W. Allport, *Personality: A Psychological Interpretation* (New York, Henry Holt and Company, Inc., 1937).

8. W. I. Thomas and Florian Znaniecki, *The Polish Peasant in Europe and America*, 5 Vols. (Chicago, The University of Chicago Press, 1918–1921).

9. For a discussion of the history and present status of attitude and its measurement, see: Melvin L. De Fleur and Frank R. Westie, "Attitude as a Scientific Concept," *Social Forces*, Vol. 42 (October, 1963), pp. 17–31.

10. A major section in one of the first textbooks in Mass Communication consists of a series of reprinted research reports dealing with audience selectivity and its basis. See: Wilbur Schramm, ed., *Mass Communications* (Urbana, University of Illinois Press, 1949), pp. 387–429.

11. The following are representative examples of research reports guided by the social categories theory: Paul F. Lazarsfeld, "Communications Research," *Current Trends in Social Psychology* (Pittsburgh, University of Pittsburgh Press, 1949), pp. 233–248; Wilbur Schramm and David White, "Age, Education and Economic Status as Factors in Newspaper Reading," Wilbur Schramm, *op. cit.*, pp. 402–412; and H. M. Beville, Jr., "The A B C D's of Radio Audiences," Wilbur Schramm, *op. cit., pp.* 413–423.

12. Auguste Comte, *op. cit.,* p. 293.

13. Harold D. Lasswell, "The Structure and Function of Communication in Society," Lyman Bryson, ed., *The Communication of Ideas* (New York, Harper and Brothers, 1948), pp. 37–51.

14. Paul F. Lazarsfeld, Bernard Berelson, and Helen Gaudet, *The People's Choice* (New York, Duell, Sloan and Pearce, 1944).

15. *Ibid.,* pp. 124–125.

16. Elihu Katz, "Communications Research and the Image of Society: Convergence of Two Research Traditions," *American Journal of Sociology*, Vol. 65, No. 5 (1960), p. 436.

17. Paul F. Lazarsfeld, Bernard Berelson, and Helen Gaudet, *op. cit.,* p. 150.

18. An excellent summary of this process is contained in: Elihu Katz, "The Two-Step Flow of Communication: An Up-to-Date Report on an Hypothesis," *Public Opinion Quarterly*, Vol. 21, No. 1 (Spring, 1957), pp. 61–78.

19. For an excellent summary of research on farm adoption see: C. Paul Marsh and A. Lee Coleman, "Group Influences and Agricultural Innovations: Some Tentative Findings and Hypotheses," *American Journal of Sociology*, Vol. 61, No. 6 (May, 1956), pp. 588–594. See also: C. M. Coughenour, "The Functioning of Farmer's Characteristics in Relation to Contacts with Media and Practice Adoption," *Rural Sociology*, Vol. 25 (September, 1960), pp. 263–297.

20. The most complete recent review of literature on such issues is: Everett M. Rogers, *Diffusion of Innovations* (New York, The Free Press of Glencoe, 1962), especially pp. 208–247.

21. Elihu Katz and Paul F. Lazarsfeld, *Personal Influence* (Glencoe, Illinois, The Free Press, 1954).

22. Melvin L. De Fleur, "The Emergence and Functioning of Opinion Leadership: Some Conditions of Informal Influence Transmission," Norman Washburne, ed., *Decisions, Values and Groups*, Vol. II (New York, The Macmillan Company, 1962), pp. 257–278.

23. Mohamed El-Assal, "Experimental Studies of Opinion Leadership: A Theoretical Formulation and Test of Selected Variables," unpublished doctoral dissertation, Indiana University, 1966.

24. Paul F. Lazarsfeld and Robert K. Merton, "Mass Communication, Popular Taste and Organized Social Action," in Lyman Bryson, ed., *The Communication of Ideas* (New York, Harper and Brothers, 1948), pp. 95–118.

25. Joseph T. Klapper, *The Effects of Mass Communication* (Glencoe, Ill., The Free Press, 1960), pp. 62–97.

26. Bernard Berelson and Patricia Salter, "Majority and Minority Americans: An Analysis of Magazine Fiction," *Public Opinion Quarterly*, Vol. 10, No. 2 (Summer, 1946), pp. 168–190.

27. For an account of this event, see: Robert K. Merton, Marjorie Fiske, and Alberta Curtis, *Mass Persuasion: The Social Psychology of a War Bond Drive* (New York, Harper and Brothers, 1946).

28. George Gerbner, "Dimensions of Violence in Television Drama," Mimeographed Report to the Mass Media Task Force, National Commission on the Causes and Prevention of Violence (forthcoming), 1969, pp. 271–358.

29. *Ibid.*, p. 279.

30. Otto N. Larsen, "Violence and the Mass Media: A Health Hazard?," Mimeographed version of paper read at the national convention of the American Society of Newspapers, Washington, D.C., April 17, 1969, p. 3.

31. Leonard Berkowitz, "The Effects of Observing Violence," *Scientific American*, Vol. 210, No. 2 (February, 1964), pp. 36–41.

32. Seymour Feshbach, "The Stimulating vs. Cathartic Effects of a Vicarious Aggressive Activity," *Journal of Abnormal and Social Psychology*, Vol. 63, No. 2, pp. 381–385. See also more recent experiments on these issues in the Mass Media Task Force Report of the National Commission on the Causes and Prevention of Violence (forthcoming).

33. Mass Media Task Force Report, *op. cit.*, p. 371.

34. Herbert Blumer and Philip Hauser, *Movies, Delinquency and Crime* (New York, The Macmillan Company, 1933).

35. Frederick C. Wertham, *Seduction of the Innocent* (New York, Rinehart and Company, Inc., 1954).

36. Thomas P. F. Hoving, "TViolence," *The Spokane Spokesman Review, This Week Magazine,* July 5, 1969, p. 5.

37. Melvin L. De Fleur and Mohamed El-Assal, *Focal Concerns in Mass Communication* (Book of Readings in Mass Communication, forthcoming, 1970).

38. Thomas P. F. Hoving, *op. cit.*, p. 5.
39. William R. Catton, Jr., "Mass Media as Producers of Effects," Mass Media Task Force Report, *op. cit.*, pp. 36–37.
40. This was the central thesis of Vance Packard in his controversial book, *The Hidden Persuaders*. He suggested that modern advertisers, using psychoanalytic mechanisms as intervening variables, were achieving powerful effects in persuading people to purchase consumer products. See: Vance Packard, *The Hidden Persuaders* (New York, David McKay Company, Inc., 1957). It was also the guiding principle underlying the work of Carl Hovland and his students in the Yale Communication and Attitude Change Program which resulted in an impressive number of publications.
41. This assumption is being called into serious question in recent studies of the relationship between attitudes and action. See: Melvin L. De Fleur and Frank R. Westie, "Verbal Attitudes and Overt Acts," *American Sociological Review*, Vol. 23, No. 6 (December, 1958), pp. 667–673.
42. Carl Hovland, Irving Janis, and Harold Kelley, *Communication and Persuasion* (New Haven, Yale University Press, 1954).
43. Irving Janis *et al.*, *Personality and Persuasibility* (New Haven, Yale University Press, 1959).
44. Leon Festinger, "Behavioral Support For Opinion Change," *Public Opinion Quarterly*, Vol. 28, No. 3 (Fall, 1964), pp. 404–417.
45. Sidney Kraus, Elaine El-Assal, and Melvin L. De Fleur, *Speech Monographs*, Vol. 33, No. 1 (March, 1966), pp. 23–29.
46. Irving Janis and Seyman Feshback, "The Effects of Fear-Arousing Communications," *Journal of Abnormal and Social Psychology*, Vol. 48 (1953), pp. 78–32.
47. Wilbur Schramm *et al.*, *Television in the Lives of Our Children* (Stanford, Calif., Stanford University Press, 1961), p. 75.
48. Joseph T. Klapper, *op. cit.*
49. Bernard Berelson, "Communications and Public Opinions," Wilbur Schramm, ed., *Mass Communications* (Urbana, University of Illinois Press, 1949), p. 500.
50. An example of such analyses would be: Herbert H. Hyman and Paul B. Sheatsley, "Some Reasons Why Information Campaigns Fail," *Public Opinion Quarterly*, Vol. 11 (Fall, 1947), pp. 412–423.
51. To illustrate, one chapter of Hovland's widely read book on *Communication and Persuasion* is entitled, "Group Membership and *Resistance* to Influence." (Italics supplied.)
52. See Kurt Lewin, "Group Decision and Social Change," in Maccoby, ed. *Readings in Social Psychology* (New York, Henry Holt and Company, Inc., 1958).
53. See Solomon E. Asch, "Effects of Group Pressure Upon the Modification and Distortion of Judgments," in Eleanor Maccoby *et al.*, *Readings in Social Psychology* (New York, Henry Holt and Company, Inc., 1958), pp. 174–183.
54. Joseph Lohman and Dietrich Reitzes, "Deliberately Organized Groups and Racial Behavior," *American Sociological Review*, Vol. 19 (June, 1954), pp. 342–344.

55. R. D. Minard, "Race Relations in the Pocahontas Coal Fields," *Journal of Social Issues,* Vol. 8, No. 1 (1952), pp. 29–44.
56. Theodore M. Newcomb, "Attitude Development as a Function of Reference Groups: The Bennington Study," Maccoby, Newcomb, and Hartley, eds., *Readings in Social Psychology* (New York, Henry Holt and Company, Inc., 1958), pp. 265–275.
57. Melvin L. De Fleur and Frank R. Westie, *op. cit.*
58. Raymond L. Gorden, "Interaction Between Attitude and the Definition of the Situation in the Expression of Opinions," *American Sociological Review,* Vol. 17 (1952), pp. 50–58.
59. Robert Merton and A. Kitt, "Contributions to the Theory of Reference Group Behavior," in Merton and Lazarsfeld, eds., *Continuities in Social Research: Studies in the Scope and Method of the American Soldier* (Glencoe, Illinois, The Free Press, 1950).
60. Margaret Mead, "Public Opinion Mechanisms among Primitive People," *Public Opinion Quarterly,* Vol. 1, No. 3 (July, 1937), pp. 5–16.
61. Margaret Mead, *ibid.*

CHAPTER VIII

1. *The Republic of Plato,* trans. Francis M. Cornford (London, Oxford University Press, 1954), pp. 68–69.
2. Examples of such claims are: Herbert Blumer and Philip Hauser, *Movies, Delinquency and Crime* (New York, The Macmillan Company, 1933), and more recently: Frederick C. Wertham, *Seduction of the Innocent* (New York, Rinehart and Company, Inc., 1954). (The latter is a bitter denunciation of comic books.)
3. Henry David Thoreau, *Walden, Or, Life in the Woods,* Vol. II (Boston and New York, Houghton Mifflin Company, 1854), pp. 148–149.
4. Thomas Carlyle, *Critical and Miscellaneous Essays,* Vol. II (London, Chapman and Hall, Ltd., 1899), p. 77.
5. Samuel Clemens, *Mark Twain's Speeches* (New York, Harper and Brothers, 1923), p. 47.
6. Quoted in Milton Ellis, Louise Pound, and George W. Spohn, *A College Book of American Literature,* Vol. I (New York, American Book Company, 1939), p. 704.
7. Talcott Parsons and Edward Shils, eds., *Toward a General Theory of Action* (New York, Harper and Row, 1962), p. 24.
8. Carl G. Hempel, "The Logic of Functional Analysis," Llewellyn Gross, *Symposium on Sociological Theory* (New York, Harper and Brothers, 1959), p. 280.
9. For a more complete analysis of these issues, see Carl Hempel, *ibid.,* pp. 271–276.
10. Stan Opotowsky, *T.V.: The Big Picture* (New York, Collier Books, 1962).

INDEX